I CHOOSE TO LIVE

I CHOOSE TO LIVE

A Self-Made Millionaire Faces Cancer

MISCHA WEISZ

WITH WADE HEMSWORTH

DUNDURN PRESS
TORONTO

Project Editor: Michael Carroll
Copy Editor: Cheryl Hawley
Design: Erin Mallory
Printer: Friesens

Library and Archives Canada Cataloguing in Publication

Weisz, Mischa
            I choose to live : a self-made millionaire faces cancer / by Mischa Weisz and Wade Hemsworth.

ISBN 978-1-55488-718-7

  1. Weisz, Mischa. 2. Pancreas--Cancer--Patients--Ontario--Hamilton-- Biography.
3. Businessmen--Ontario--Hamilton--Biography. 4. Children of Holocaust survivors--Ontario--Hamilton--
Biography. I. Hemsworth, Wade, 1965- II. Title.

RC280.P25W44 2009   362.196'994370092   C2009-905574-0

1 2 3 4 5   13 12 11 10 09

Conseil des Arts du Canada   Canada Council for the Arts   Canada   ONTARIO ARTS COUNCIL CONSEIL DES ARTS DE L'ONTARIO

We acknowledge the support of the **Canada Council for the Arts** and the **Ontario Arts Council** for our publishing program. We also acknowledge the financial support of the **Government of Canada** through the **Book Publishing Industry Development Program** and **The Association for the Export of Canadian Books**, and the **Government of Ontario** through the **Ontario Book Publishers Tax Credit** program, and the **Ontario Media Development Corporation.**

Care has been taken to trace the ownership of copyright material used in this book. The author and the publisher welcome any information enabling them to rectify any references or credits in subsequent editions.

                                                                                                    J. Kirk Howard, President

Printed and bound in Canada.
www.dundurn.com

Dundurn Press
3 Church Street, Suite 500
Toronto, Ontario, Canada
M5E 1M2

Gazelle Book Services Limited
White Cross Mills
High Town, Lancaster, England
LA1 4XS

Dundurn Press
2250 Military Road
Tonawanda, NY
U.S.A. 14150

To my children, Danielle and Nathan. Writing this book is my way of staying with you long after I am gone. You have inspired me to do my very best, and I am deeply proud to be your father. I love you completely and always.

CONTENTS

INTRODUCTION
A Conversation Between Friends

Early Evening, June 11, 2009

An enormous terracotta teapot is steaming on the stove, crammed with a simmering nest of stems, stalks, and berries. The exhaust fan overhead is working hard, but cannot overcome the persistent stench of the Chinese medicinal tea that is designed to keep Mischa Weisz alive.

He and two boyhood friends, the three of them now in their fifties, have gathered in the eat-in kitchen of Mischa's executive home in suburban Ancaster, on the outskirts of Hamilton, Ontario.

On one side of the long pine table is Paul Buckle, who manages the municipal animal control department. He is sitting closest to the back door so that he can slip out to the back step and smoke, keeping the door open so he never has to leave the conversation. Burly and gravel voiced, Paul wears his graying whiskers halfway between long stubble and a short beard. In contrast to his appearance, he is alternately pensive and playfully provocative, drawing ably from a deep vocabulary and sipping from a tumbler of Scotch.

Opposite Paul is Frank Helt, investment banker. Trim and tanned, he has taken off his suit jacket, but his white shirt, with its monogrammed French cuffs, is still crisp. Straightforward and sincere, he is composed and thoughtful as he balances fine detail against broad context, choosing his words with care. The way he chides and advocates for Mischa suggests he is an older-brother figure to his friend of more than forty years. Frank and Paul, and their wives Linda and Jackie, are, like Mischa's wife Connie and his brother Guido and Guido's wife Bonnie, part of a trusted circle of family and friends who have long served to smooth Mischa's sharper edges, to curb his more drastic impulses, sometimes to act as interpreters for the complex man whom they all love in different ways.

At the end of the table, Mischa himself is uncharacteristically quiet. At this point, he is about a year-and-a-half past the five month prognosis he got when doctors diagnosed him with terminal pancreatic cancer. Medically he is very ill, yet personally he appears robust, his eyes shining with intensity. Since he got the news he has been pushing the gas pedal of his life right to the floor, with no idea and not much concern over how much is really left in the tank.

All of Mischa's fifty-three years have prepared him for this point. He has learned, in life and in business, to trust his own wits and trained himself to treat even the most deeply personal, and sometimes tragic, problems logically and nearly objectively. A proudly self-taught entrepreneur, he has done well enough in the electronic banking business to count his wealth in the millions of dollars, and since selling his company a month earlier has happily indulged his love of gambling and thirst for science fiction, while investing carefully in his health care and his legacy. He is telling his life's story as a book and in a documentary film. He values closure, and is tying up all his loose ends while he can. He has already donated half a million dollars to the YMCA, in the hope of giving kids a fairer start in life, and has set aside more money for charity in his will.

He appears to be afraid of nothing, except for leaving the people closest to him, and in particular he wants to make sure that after he is gone his daughter and son have the best approximation of a father that he can provide.

Tonight, he relaxes in a golf shirt and sweatpants, cupping his mug of awful tea and savouring the sounds of his two best friends taking turns teasing him and explaining why they treasure him.

Paul: If you talk to any ten people about what Mischa is like, you're going to get ten different answers. What has kept the three of us coming back for more over the years is the fun, circumstantial stuff.

We have enough history that there's always a touchstone, an aspect of the familiar, but there are also enough differences between Mischa and Frank and me that you never know what's going to happen next.

Mischa is an intensely private person. Nobody, as far as I know, has complete access to Mischa Weisz. He has always been one of these people who very carefully guards his heart, and when you do finally get a piece of that you realize there is value there that other people might not be seeing, because he finds it so hard to let anyone in to begin with. And the piece that Frank gets is a little different from the one I get, which is different from the pieces that he gives to the other people who are close to him in his life. Nobody ever sees the same guy, and nobody, as far as I know, has seen all of him.

As a result, we don't all necessarily respond to him in the same way, either. He comes off as being pretty up front and he says these outrageous things, and if you're foolish you'll walk away thinking that's what he really believes, when in fact he's saying them just to see what you'll do. He wants to see where you're coming from. He enjoys watching the rest of us respond, too. That's the performer in him. I think that the people who get to know him realize that the more you think you know, the more you realize you don't know about him.

Frank: It was 1967, and I was ten years old. I was one of five children in my family, living on Aberdeen Avenue near Locke Street, a busy corner in an older residential section of Hamilton with big brick houses and lots of trees.

Mischa's family moved in beside us one day. Why we started to hang out, I don't know. I had strict parents and Mischa had strict parents, so we both knew what it was like to live with a lot of rules. Mischa's dad was a music teacher and he wasn't allowed to make noise in or near his house while his dad was giving lessons, which seemed to be most of the time.

Mischa's younger brother, Guido, was closer to my age, but I was drawn to Mischa. He had this affinity for electronic gizmos and train sets in the basement, and I found that stuff kind of cool. I didn't have a transistor radio, but Mischa had a crystal radio set hooked up to the radiator in his room, and he could tune in all sorts of stuff. I found that fascinating, and we formed an instant bond.

It wasn't your usual connection between two kids. We didn't play sports together, we didn't go to the same school, and we didn't have the same friends, but there was this novelty to him that made him a little different and appealing.

We used to watch sports every Saturday — ABC's *Wide World of Sports* — at my house and we would have lunch.

I was almost never in Mischa's house, because it had to be very quiet. We couldn't even play ball in the driveway because the noise would interrupt the lessons, so Mischa was always over at our place. That was the beginning of what would become a very long-term relationship.

Mischa was a little quirky. He was nearly two years older than me. By thirteen he was shaving. There were curiosities about him that made him stand out differently and I found him interesting. Mischa had a wonderful affinity for music. He is an accomplished pianist and pretty good flautist. He picked up a guitar and simply taught himself. I couldn't do that. I'm very left brain, very logical. He's very right brain, very creative. Maybe that was part of the appeal.

Even today, on New Year's Eve when we meet up at somebody's house, I always ask him to play the piano. I think the way he sees music is the way he sees technology. With the musical aptitude he got from his family, he took his talent to a whole different platform — technology — and that's where he found his success. He was thinking outside the box while other people were thinking more conventionally.

We are yin and yang as friends. We respect each other's differences, so we're never in conflict.

Paul: Mischa and I first ran into each other in 1968, at the YMCA day camp in downtown Hamilton. I was living in the east end then and he was in the west end.

Here was this other kid who wasn't anything extraordinary. He wasn't good at sports. He hated being bitten by mosquitoes. We had that in common: neither of us really wanted to be there at that time. We had better things, we thought, that we could be doing, but of course we were having a better time than we realized or admitted.

At that juncture, it never really occurred to either one of us that we'd ever see the other again. We were just camp buddies. I went back to the east end and he went back to his home in the southwest. My mother liked to move — I think my father went along with it as a way to avoid painting — and I ended up moving out to Aberdeen Avenue the next year and suddenly there was Mischa, the kid I had been buddies with in camp. We lived down at the other end of Aberdeen, near the golf course and the Westinghouse factory, and we started hanging out. He showed me around and told me what was what. We went to Westdale Secondary School together and my house was on the way.

He'd call on me and I'd invariably be running late and he'd be hustling me along because he never wanted to be late. I was there for grade nine and partway through grade ten, and by the time we moved again, we were solid friends.

What kept us connected was that at the time on Aberdeen Avenue there was a small Unitarian church in a house next to Mischa's place. My father was a cop and he was afraid of where I was going in life because I wanted to grow long hair and smoke dope. He had some friends who went to the Unitarian church and thought he'd send me there, to be part of their youth group. He didn't want to send me to a Catholic group because that would be too much, but he figured the Unitarian option would still help me straighten out.

They had a youth group called LRY, which stood for Liberal Religious Youth, and back in those days they used to say, "Stress the 'liberal', not the 'religious.'" At the time, they used to say some U.S. chapters of the LRY were on the FBI's list of subversive groups. I have no idea whether or not that was true, but it sounded great to us at the time. Who belonged to this group but Mischa. Every Thursday or Friday night I'd show up, even after we moved. A lot of the kids who were part of that group became our friends.

Little did our parents know what it was really like. It was hardly religious at all. It was more hippie. It was a very liberal take on society. We went away to camp. They called it Unicamp. The camp nurse would give you condoms if you were smart enough to ask. By the time my father found out how ungoverned we really were it was too late. We'd go away to all these conferences and run coffee houses to pay our way. It was a pretty interesting way to grow up.

It turned out Mischa and I both had an interest in science fiction and we've been exchanging books ever since. We haven't maintained as consistent a relationship as he and Frank have over the years. We'd kind of come and go, but always come back together. Later, when we moved out of our parents' houses, we ended up in the same apartment highrise on the outer edge of downtown Hamilton, just a few floors apart.

We both had an interest in CB radios and he was into the ham radio end of things, and we'd build stereos. I particularly remember building a set of speakers, with Mischa advising me on how to put them together. He told me what I should do and it worked like a charm, but as it turned out I hadn't bought enough screws to hold all the speakers in their cabinets. Mischa said, "I know where we can get some screws." We went down to the laundry room and stole one screw from each of the dryers. We didn't ravage any one dryer, but we took one screw that was more or less ornamental from each of the dryers and that gave us just enough to finish the job.

I like the story because it shows that not only was he creative, but he had this incredible memory. He knew not only where we could get enough screws, but that they would be the right size. It was like he had had a mental inventory of available screws and went through it to recall which ones would be the right size for the job.

Frank: The lottery ticket is probably our best story. Initially I was quite upset, but three or four days later I realized what a great joke it had been, and have continued, in my own mind, to say what a great joke it was.

I had won $5,000 in the old Wintario lottery sometime in the late 1970s, around five years before I got married, and I know Mischa was a little bit envious. We both played the lotteries then quite a bit. When I won the money, I bought a couch — I still have it today — and a table and a chair. I also bought pizza and beer and took it over to Mischa's apartment. We all used to hang out there, since he was the first guy to move out of the house.

Back then, before they announced the numbers on the radio and long before the Internet, you could get the winning numbers by calling a hotline. I always forgot the number, but Mischa, being the way he is, had memorized it. I called him all the time to get the numbers. One day, I left my wallet over at his apartment with my lottery ticket in it, and picked it up the next day.

After the draw, I called him up to get the winning numbers. As he read them out, they matched my ticket perfectly. I had won $100,000! I was on the phone in the kitchen of my future wife Linda's house. I screamed that I had won the jackpot. Linda knew Mischa, and she said it was impossible.

Now, being a little conniving, I'm sure Mischa had opened my wallet up, found the ticket and thought about what he could do with it, in exactly the same way he had dreamed up what to do with the screws in the dryers. Well, he had copied down the numbers from my ticket, and when I called to ask him for the winning numbers, he just read my own numbers back to me.

I am a very trusting person. If somebody tells me something, I believe it. I believed Mischa. I thought I had won the lottery. Linda didn't believe Mischa. She tried calling him back, but he had taken the phone off the hook. Finally, maybe two hours later, we got him on the line and he admitted it. For two hours, I had thought I was rich. I was pissed off for a day or two, but when I circled back on that experience, I realized that he'd given me something nobody else could ever give me: the feeling that I'd won the lottery. As opposed to thinking "what an asshole," as I did for the first little while, I later came to be happy to have had such a rush.

I had been working at a down-and-out job right out of university, and I had thought, "This is it". Thank God I wasn't in a bar at the time, or I would have bought drinks for everybody.

Mischa and I have been friends consistently through the last forty-two years, though it has come and gone. There were times when I went my way and he went his way, but there was always New Year's Eve and always one week in the summer when we would reunite. Because we had these smaller pieces out of an entire year, neither of us would get overwhelmed by somebody's personality or character. You could take it, enjoy it, embrace it, and just leave it. We would hang around in the summers when we were teens. We would drink, we would smoke, we would party together, and in the fall we went to different schools. I went to the Catholic high school, St. Mary's, and Mischa went to the public high school in our end of the city, Westdale.

Our friendship wasn't based on commitments or work. It was based on all the fun stuff. That kept us together. We had commonalities, in that we both wanted to succeed. My upbringing was also a strict upbringing, and we wanted to show our parents we could do something. We had this drive to be successful. Later, business ideas and business ventures kept us together.

All three of us would go camping. That was someplace where you could be on your own and do everything you wanted. Mischa, for his part, would fumigate the entire area around our campsite. I'm not talking about spraying a can of Raid. He had one of those pumps and would spray insecticide on everything. It's dark humour, but I like to joke that it's probably why he's sick today.

Maybe the magic in a relationship like that was that whenever we pissed each other off, nobody ever had to forgive anybody. It just disappeared. You would just move on when you saw each other the next time. Maybe that's what guys do.

Paul: To me, Mischa has always been a guy who's looked at things with just enough of a twist to develop a different perspective. I think he was the first person to force me to do that. He has always forced me to step back and take a look at everything from a second perspective and see it a different way. Now I do it with everybody, but I think if I never would have met Mischa, I would never have learned to do that, and I would have missed an awful lot.

There were a lot of people who knew what was going to happen in the whole automated banking industry around the time that Mischa knew it. They knew the government was getting ready to open it up to competition, but there were not a lot of other people who were willing to take a risk on it, and take advantage of it. Mischa was prepared to trust himself and risk what little he had to exploit the opportunity. He had to work hard on it, but he made it pay like nobody else.

Mischa takes these really strange risks — ones that other people wouldn't take or that wouldn't occur to other people to be worth taking. He's not averse to risk and this is also the case in the way he's dealing with his cancer. Most people I know who are diagnosed with Stage IV cancer accept whatever their oncologists say and carry on until they die somewhere close to their deadline.

Mischa has taken on the ultimate risk and merged Western, Eastern, and alternative forms of treatment, and put them together in an unconventional way, having no idea of what the outcome will be, or whether it will be beneficial. In his mind, it's worth the risk to try it. The question now is: has he lasted nearly two years when they said he would last five months because he saw something other people didn't see and was prepared to take the risk, or because he saw something that other people had seen but weren't willing to risk? Or has he simply won the oncology jackpot by living this long? We'll never know. What we do know is that he has taken the risk and for whatever reason, it has paid off in the same way it did with the independent bank machines.

The key element here is not why he has been able to manage to survive so long, but what it demonstrates about the type of personality you're dealing with. This is a person who isn't necessarily willing to follow the crowd. He listens to the experts and respects them, but he's also someone who will say, "I'm going to try it this way because I might get a different result, so I think it's worth the risk." Maybe it's paying off. Who knows? But the key element is that he has taken the risk.

Frank: I've been in business with Mischa and I've seen him in operation. He is one of these people who is a true CEO. He's kind of rough around the edges and takes input from people around him who are experts, but then he decides what he's going to do with it.

With his company, he was able to do that. He had an initial vision and gathered input from many sources, and kept going to the next step. The value side of that is that Mischa was an underdog. He has always had something to prove. Mischa's legacy might be that he allowed other underdogs to achieve.

There was a kid in our neighbourhood once who had found a little black puppy that had been abandoned. He was looking for somebody to take the dog. My parents wouldn't let me have it. Nobody's parents would let them have it, even though every kid on the street wanted it. Mischa fought his parents and got to keep that dog and they had it for many years. It was truly an underdog situation.

He had taken that dog and given it the chance at a normal life.

Take that forward to Mischa's work in his company. If you look at the people who made up his company, it was filled with people others might not have believed in. His first employee had a physical disability that other people might not have seen past, but he had a wonderful mind and needed an opportunity. Mischa hired him and gave him a chance, and he did very well. There was another fellow who came in who was a programmer who was also pretty far outside the standard business model, both in look and demeanour. He was a Trekkie, but he was bright and skilled. He never had formal training in his field, but he did a great job and he moved up in the company. When you go through the roster of Mischa's employees, they were all extremely capable, but in many cases you had to work to see it, and believe they could do the job. They weren't your typical college and university grads. Many of them are still there under the new owners. He would give the opportunity to an unconventional person and that person would thrive.

I think Mischa likes the limelight. He likes the attention he gets at the casino. He likes the attention he gets from making a philanthropic gift. But what he did there was not for attention. He just did it because giving people a chance was the right thing to do. His legacy is the value he has contributed, hands on, to people's lives. Some of them ended up making salaries they never would have dreamed of making.

That's the CEO side of Mischa: bringing these bright minds together and allowing them to thrive and, in turn, allowing his business to thrive. What he is doing now is bringing great people together to fight his cancer using the same open mind and trying things that other people wouldn't try. Now everybody's wondering if there's more to this idea.

He's also bringing lot of attention to the fight against cancer by doing this book, and with the movie he's having made. He's doing this to help stroke his ego a little bit, which probably helps trigger those endorphins that help to keep him healthy, but there is also true value in the lessons of his life. I sense that Mischa's true worth is in giving something to other people.

I'm methodical. He's a maverick. We get along well together because I can envy his gutsy calls and he can look at my practicality and realize there is merit in that. Mischa has real horseshoes in his back pocket. It has stood him well in taking risks that most people won't take. I am often the little whisper in his ear telling him he might want to put the parachute on before he jumps out of the plane. He calls me and asks what I think of something and I'll tell him the reasons not to do it and he'll say, "You're full of shit," and do it anyway. I do my job, but he makes his own decisions. He shoots from the hip. In many cases, I'm left wondering, "How the heck did that happen?" He wanted to buy MGM stock recently and I told him about all the signs that were indicating it wasn't a good idea. At the end of the day, it multiplied in value and he sold it and made a quick $50,000.

He has always been the one who was the underdog and accomplished and overcame. That has been all through his life. It was that way with school, which was hard for him. When it comes to cancer, he shows us that you don't have to accept it. You don't have to roll up in a ball and wither away.

He has grown a business and been successful handled adversity in his life and now he's not settling for the idea of dying of cancer.

Paul: I was at home when I got a call from a mutual friend who asked me if I'd heard about Mischa being sick. At that point, Mischa and I hadn't talked for several years, so I said no, I hadn't. I thought about it maybe ten minutes, and I called him.

"Listen. I hear you're not well."

"Yeah. I have Stage IV pancreatic cancer."

"Well, whatever issues we had, let's let bygones be bygones, and carry on from here."

He agreed.

When we were in our twenties, Mischa had quit smoking and I hadn't. We were having this drunken argument over the kitchen table as a result of his grabbing hold of the chalice of proper living and good health. We were arguing over who would outlast the other. We made a bet to the tune of $10,000. We bet that whoever died first would have to have his estate pay the survivor $10,000.

He was convinced that, by virtue of having quit smoking, he was going to outlast the rest of us. We joked about it over the years. He was always doing things to improve his health. He hired a personal trainer and he bought all this exercise equipment. I've always been a hard-drinking, hard-smoking guy, completely unconcerned with any of that sort of stuff.

So I hear the guy is dying and I call him up and make my amends. He tells me there's a get-together with some of his other friends and invites me.

My wife Jackie told me not to do it, but I walk in, and the first words I say are, "You remember that $10,000 bet?"

"Yes."

"It looks like you'll be paying it."

He shoots right back: "How do you know I won't take you out first?"

It's always been that way with us: kind of rough and tumble.

He doesn't want a lot of sympathy. He wants understanding and compassion, and he wants us to understand how he plans to play out the rest of his life. At the same time, he's never been one to suffer other people being maudlin. My perception of him has always been that he is one to look a problem in the eye and spit in its face.

I think he's treating the disease in the same way. He views it as a separate entity and he views it as an opponent. He wants to look death in the eye and spit in its face. So the last thing we should be doing as his friends is saying, "Oh, poor Mischa." He sets the tone. This is Mischa's thing. For the most part, we all have a chance to set the tone from time to time. Mischa is setting it now.

Frank: Mischa and I are in active, day-to-day contact. My dad had been his doctor for a long time, and Mischa and I have frequently talked about his health. A few years ago, he started having trouble with his blood sugar and I kept suggesting he get more tests.

About two years ago, he told me he'd found a lump in his abdomen, and I said he should get it checked immediately.

Starting with the period when his blood sugar had started to go haywire, when Mischa was getting all these tests done he would constantly page me on my BlackBerry. I have kept every one of his messages and uploaded them to my laptop. I have hundreds and hundreds of them, and if you were to read them you'd see them getting darker and darker. We had already lost two friends to pancreatic cancer, and we thought there was no way it could be happening to him.

When he finally found out, he sent me a message that said, simply, "It's not good. It's really not good."

I called him and he had a bit of a crack in his voice, and he said he couldn't talk right then. I hung up and immediately I got scared. I phoned my wife and I remember coming home that night and saying, "God, this year is going to be miserable for all of us," because we thought he was going to die.

That lasted about an hour and then we started making phone calls. We called doctors and surgeons we knew and got his file moved up the queue. Instead of us all dwelling on some foregone conclusion, we all got active and immediately felt better. We were moving the clock so much faster than what usually happens in Ontario.

Paul: It was fascinating to witness Frank and Mischa interacting and working out the plan. They were working to buy bits of time here and there, and hoping that the longer they could extend things, the better chance that new ideas would come down the pike and buy more time. Frank was working out this game plan from the very get-go. It was very interesting to watch the interplay between them. Frank was moving Mischa to pursue a course of action that would give him some control over his destiny. At the same time, Frank was also helping himself in terms of what was happening to his friend. With Mischa responding positively to Frank's encouragement, it became a feedback loop. Frank was helping Mischa, and that would help Frank, and so on. It was wild to watch it go on in the first few months. Did it make a difference? Probably.

Frank: Mischa got it rolling, and we all encouraged him. Mischa got more creative. He knew about the Block Center, a private institution in the States where they do complementary cancer treatment. We said, why not? It could help, and it's certainly not going to hurt anything. Then he tried light therapy, alkaline water, and even a person who kind of hovered over him. He has tried all this stuff that's kind of wild and far out there, but it has made him feel good.

Mischa puts the cancer in a box and puts the box in a closet and lives his life the way he wants to. Whether it's winning at the casino or selling his company, or buying stocks and making money, all these things keep him up. I couldn't to it. I am in awe of Mischa's resolve. Nobody wants to die, but he's not afraid to die. That may come from his lineage and what his Jewish ancestors have endured over time. At the same time he also has a sense that death is finite and when it's over, it's over, and there is no anxiousness over having to repent. He doesn't worry about that because it's not part of his world. The way he sees it, when he's dead, he's dead, so nothing he does is going to come back and haunt him. He's not afraid of death.

I am not ready to talk about his early death as a foregone conclusion. It's not proven. There are miracles all around us, including people who had terminal illnesses and are alive and well today. Whenever his day comes, he is very accepting of the inevitable, and that has kept him from quivering in his journey through what he has to go through to get there.

I know Mischa has a mixed perception of his parents. I've known his parents all my life, and I have known them from a different perspective than Mischa has. I know it's possible, from my own life, for people to have very different perspectives on the same person. I know his parents went through hell in the war. His father has only told me a little, but he has told me enough for me to know it was a very difficult experience to have and to process.

I think the fact that Mischa comes from a line of survivors has something to do with the fact that he has survived as long as has and done as well as he has. It's not just his parents, but his grandmother, who lived to 103. I don't know if it is pure human genetics that give you a physical and internal drive not to let things get you down, or if your environment comes into play. In the early stages of life, you take after what your parents model and what they give you genetically. His parents were brought up in a certain world and they survived. His dad was a tough son of a bitch and he survived, and he may have passed some of that to Mischa. That might be the legacy his parents gave him: that he wanted to prove to them he could be successful no matter what they said, and he did it.

Paul: I think there's an element of nurture and nature in it, and an element of challenge. I don't think that today he's out to prove anything to his parents. I think he's beyond that, but initially, like we all do, he tried to be successful. It's a form of rebellion.

Aren't we all looking for some measure of our own worth? Whether the yardstick is held by our parents, or our friends, or by society in general, we're all looking for some external confirmation of our own value. It's all part of the whole affiliation-motivation dynamic that drives us to be seen as valuable by some kind of group so our DNA doesn't get lost.

I agree with Frank to some extent, but there are significant differences, too.

Mischa's family would have survived the gulag and the pogroms and the Holocaust by flying under the radar. Mischa is surviving by ignoring the radar completely. Under it, over it, he doesn't care about it. He is completely disregarding the radar. I think his willingness to reject conventional thinking has a lot to do with his ability to survive.

The perfect CEO surrounds himself with experts, gathers their advice, and then decides how much of it to accept before he chooses his own way. The gift is in being able to filter information and winnow the wheat from the chaff. That is part of his strength.

Regardless of the circumstances, he has always wanted to live his life to the fullest and he has always wanted a measure of control over how it plays out. This isn't really that much different. This is merely a variation on the same theme. Mischa's plans, as I know them, are to meet the demands that his condition requires: he drinks that disgusting tea because he has to, but he doesn't deny himself the things he is allowed to have. He has not become a Spartan or a Zen monk.

He is always looking to that next little lift.

He has this innate desire to grab life with both hands and take big bites out of things. Robert Heinlein said moderation is for monks. If you really want to live life, grab it with both hands. I think Mischa has always seen it that way. He was the first one of us with his own apartment. He has always been one of those people who likes to live life large. That may well be one of the things that help him to survive. He is not letting stress and concerns over his mortality push him into his room to feel sorry for himself. He is pursuing the battle against cancer with a vengeance, but at the same time that's not his sole focus. He's also having a good time. Maybe we should all be taking a lesson from that, but who knows?

Frank: I'll miss our interactions. There is a chunk of my life that is Mischa that will become a void. There will always be the memories and the stories. My days will be less cluttered. I will be less distracted. But those are things I have looked forward to that will immediately register as a profound loss when they're gone. There are things that I like doing with him and I won't have him to do them with any more.

I started writing his eulogy on my BlackBerry six or eight weeks after he was diagnosed and I have been working on it ever since. I've had to do two eulogies in my life, and I was proud to be asked. When I asked for counsel on how to do it, the best advice I got was to talk about what you know. Other people can talk about what they know. I am going to talk about my relationship with Mischa. I am going to talk about him and that crystal radio set, I am going to talk about him standing on the edge of the Niagara Escarpment looking out over Hamilton with his walkie-talkie that he has supercharged and put a twelve-foot aerial on, and he's talking to people miles away. It all led to what he became.

This book, as far as I can see, is motivational. You think you've got a challenge in business? Look at what he has done in his business, and then gone on to fight his cancer in this way. Suddenly your own business problems look pretty insignificant when you see what this guy has to fight.

Paul: I don't think this is about telling you how to live or deal with your own cancer. I don't think it's a dying man's attempt to tell his story. My sense is that this is more about the fact that we all have choices. We can choose to roll up into a ball and feel sorry for ourselves or we can choose to do something about it. When we make the choice between those two, a whole cornucopia of other options opens up. The thing with Mischa is that you've always got a choice. It doesn't matter if you have cancer. It doesn't matter if your wife left you, or your dog died, or your truck doesn't work: you've got choices. You can take some control of what you're going to do next. That has always been part of Mischa's philosophy. He always says, "Okay. What's next?"

CHAPTER 1
Refusing to Die on Schedule

I was boxing. I wanted to be in shape. I'd always had a tummy. I'm five foot six, and I was up to 220 pounds at one point. I was boxing for exercise — not hitting other people — and I felt this mass on the right side of my stomach, and it hurt. I thought it was a hernia. It was solid, about the size of my fist.

I went to my doctor, and the first thing he said was, "What the hell is that?" He sent me for an ultrasound and it didn't look like there was anything wrong, but there was all this fluid building up in my abdomen and as soon as you hear that, it's serious. At that point, my doctor told me it looked like I had pancreatic cancer, which is a very aggressive type of cancer.

Not long after that, I learned that surgery was not an option and that I could expect to live four or five months. That was two years ago, and I am still here. I am not in denial, but I refuse to die on schedule. I have used just about every form of treatment available: Western, Eastern, and alternative. I meditate every day. I have changed my diet and changed my outlook. I sold my company and now I indulge myself in everything I want, except for the things that will harm me, and even then I sometimes cheat a little.

I have tied up all the loose ends of my life that were in my power to tidy up, and I am at peace with the rest. I have given away a chunk of my fortune to charity and plan to give more in my estate. I know my children will be looked after financially, and I have commissioned a documentary film and I'm doing this book to leave them some kind of legacy. If I'm not going to be around, I want them to know who Mischa Weisz was. I want them to understand the essence of Mischa Weisz, the spirit. Decades from now, some descendants of mine may wonder why little Johnny is acting so crazy or why he's so determined, and they can realize he's just like his great-great-great-grandfather Mischa. Maybe that spirit will carry on.

My children and my parents love each other, but they don't have the close relationship that many grandparents and grandchildren have, and my kids know that my relationship with my parents is complicated. I need to find a way to let my children and their children and their grandchildren know why that is. When it comes to family, people always want the perfection that includes a long, unbroken connection. I am hoping that through the book they'll get an idea of what has happened.

In the time since my diagnosis, I have tried to connect better with my kids, been married, gambled, and golfed to my heart's content, made money in the stock market, slept-in, travelled, and learned fly-fishing. I have been pierced, drained, drugged, opened up, and sewn back up again.

I can't say for sure why I am still here, but I am content knowing that I am doing everything I possibly can, not just to stay alive but to live in the fullest sense of living.

An old friend who died many, many years ago said something to me, and it made so much sense that I have never forgotten it: "If you have to fart, fart."

That's what I've been doing all my life: farting. Doing what I needed to do to get to where I needed to go. Sometimes I didn't even know where I was going, but I just went. At the end of the day, it was okay. I've learned that if you don't do anything, nothing happens. So many people throughout history have sat and expected something to happen. It doesn't work that way. You, as an individual, have to make things happen. I have proven time and time again that I can do shit and make things happen.

Everybody tells me that I'm a truly unique and complex person. I've heard it a thousand times, and I have never really known what they meant. Even my brother Guido says I am complex, but I don't feel that way. My friend Paul says I am guarded, but I don't see it. I see myself as an open book. I am not trying to hold anything back.

I am a combination of everything, I guess. I try to be a humanitarian, but I can be a bit of an asshole. I'm not perfect, but I try to have fun with life and sometimes that confuses people.

Humour is a major part of my life and a significant factor in my survival. I'm more secure today than I was when I was younger. Humour has always been a good way of masking my insecurities. I also think it's healthy to laugh whenever you can, especially when life gets too serious. I can make fun of anyone, including myself, at any time. I like making people laugh. Humour gives you licence to get away with saying and doing a lot of things you could never get away with otherwise. It lets you tell the truth without causing pain. It grabs people's attention in a way that nothing else can do. For me, entertaining others with humour is also a way of entertaining myself.

I try to approach my illness with a little mischief, too. I don't see it as a choice. You can be sad and down about what's happening to you, or you can try to make light of it.

I've done so much in my life, and gathered so much information, that I have developed a kind of a panoramic view of society. I understand people. I can often figure out what they are going to say before they say it.

By now, I understand this world very well. That sounds bizarre, I know, but I'm confident that I do. I understand it more than I understand myself, though I'm at peace with myself. People tell me I'm very smart, but they also say I'm off the wall.

They also say I'm arrogant, or caustic, or selfish. I find myself very straightforward and I simply shoot from the hip and say what I want to say. That's the way I am.

In a way, I am putting together this book in the hope that one day I'll pick it up and figure out who the hell I really am.

One thing I know for sure is that my life should be seen as a success story, not a tragedy. Nowhere close. I raised two children successfully, came though many challenges, and learned to live with my cancer. I think it's a triumph all the way.

I am definitely a member of the TV generation. The TV was a babysitter, and its characters were my childhood friends. Today I have a TV screen the size of a pool table and I watch it whenever I can. I grew up idealizing the families I saw on shows such as *Leave It to Beaver* and *My Three Sons*, and I wondered why my family seemed so different. I watched *Star Trek* with my dad and brother when I was a kid, and I still love science fiction, and so does Guido. We both liked it for the characters and situations. Watching that show led him to study sociology. It led me to admire strong leadership. My two favourite characters from *Star Trek* are Captain Kirk from the original series and Captain Picard from *The Next Generation*, because they are naturally powerful. I like how they can control situations and make things happen. I respect that. I like strong leadership. I even took some of the philosophy behind *Star Trek* for running my company. The premise was that if you had a good crew, you didn't need to be on the bridge.

I thought my staff should be able to run the ship while I was in the ready room, reading books. My belief was, "If I can't have people who I can tell, 'Make it so,' what the fuck am I paying them for?"

I am what I like to call a memory disposer. If it doesn't make me happy and isn't relevant and it's been a while, I dispose of it, just like taping over a videotape you don't ever want to watch again.

It's my fiction. I want to be happy, and if something doesn't make me happy, then, even as I'm thinking about it, I watch myself from the outside thinking about it. It's a fucked up thing. It's like I'm inside myself being me while I am also outside myself observing myself, so I do my best to untangle it all by getting rid of the problem.

I think I want to live in this perfect little world and have a nice little family, like you see on TV. That's probably one of the reasons I fought for the custody of my children when my first wife and I divorced: to prove that such an entity could exist. I am very happy I did that and I am very proud of it.

After trying hard to find it, I have come to accept that there is no *Leave It to Beaver* family for me, or for anyone. But there are happy families, and that is what I have done my best to create.

My son, Nathan, showed up with his girlfriend while the movie crew was here shooting the documentary about my life. He wanted to be interviewed, and that made me very happy. I had said he could come if he wanted, but he's nineteen, so he hardly shows up for anything, so that made me very happy when he came. And he was with his girlfriend, and that's important, too, because it tells me that he wants her to be part of this time and to know where he comes from. All it took was him deciding to drop by, and I could feel the circle closing, because he was taking the time to come up. It was important to him and it was good for him. It's not always easy for fathers and sons to be close, especially at his age, but he is trying to find a way that he's comfortable with, and that's good. I wanted him to do it on his terms, because if I forced it, it wouldn't work.

Soon I am going to take him to Victoria with me for three days to see my daughter, his big sister, Danielle. I think it's very good. Danielle will be working some of the time we're there, so Nathan and I will also have some time of our own, and I'm looking forward to that.

What I am most excited about is that the three of us will be together like we were when they were kids and we'd go camping or to Disney World.

Everybody knows what point I'm at in my life, but I think it will be no different from any other trip and, honestly, I don't want it to be. We may talk about what things are going on in my life. We may talk about what happens when I die, but overall, there's only so much to talk about on that subject. Death is death.

All I want is for us to spend some time together. I need happy memories and I need them to have happy memories.

This is a rich time of life for me. I told my friends that I am the luckiest guy in the whole wide world in one sense: I couldn't handle watching them die. I would be a complete and total mess, having known and depended on some of them for more than forty years. I am at the pinnacle of my life, knowing I am close to the end, but savouring what I have. It's sort of like the cowboy in the Westerns who gets shot sixty-seven times before he falls down.

We are all born and we all die, and I see the life we live as a line between those two points. When I meet someone new, I might say, "Hello, it's nice to meet you," and never see that person again, or I could strike up a friendship with that person and we could stay in touch. That shifts my line and it shifts the other person's line a little bit. You have a lot of these experiences, and the more you have, the more interesting your life's line looks. You're given a lot of opportunities and if you don't take those opportunities, then your life is not enriched. I truly believe that. You can call it holy or not, but I think we're all given these opportunities.

I have looked at other stories about people with terminal cancer, like *The Last Lecture* video and Farrah Fawcett's documentary, and they seem to invite sympathy or pity. The reality is you have cancer. Deal with it and make the best of it. That's what's important. I do not want to have someone who looks at my story thinking, "Let's watch Mischa disappear and die." I am going to disappear and die. That's just a fact. I don't want people staring at me, watching and wringing their hands while I draw my last breaths. That's not what it's about. My goal is to live right up until the moment of death. Most people don't look at it like that. We all die. When people hear cancer, they think death, and start getting ready for death. I'm not getting ready for death. I know it's going to happen one day, but I am going to live until then. I am having fun. I'll probably be at the casino, and with my luck I'll hit the big jackpot one minute before I die and not be able to do anything with it.

When people read this book, I want them to finish it believing that you can succeed in life if you put your mind to it. You have to have certain qualities to succeed, most of all, determination. Not that I struggled, but I always had walls in my face. I overcame them. At the end of the day what I'd like to teach people is that you can win at anything you want.

What I am hoping is that people get some hope and inspiration from my book. I hope to show them, here is a person who tried honestly to do the right things and live life the right way. I wasn't perfect at it and I never will be perfect at it. I like using shock in my life. I'm a little fucked up and weird. I know that. But it's okay. I hope people who read it will have a few laughs. I'd like people to feel a little sentimental. I'd like them to be touched. Most of all, I want them to see they can do the same things and more with their own lives.

The lesson is simple: you're in control of your destiny. You really are. We talk about that line from A to Z that represents your life. You control that line. If you decide not to intersect with someone or some thing and change that line a little bit, that's up to you. Those lines are opportunities. You'll end up at the end of your line no matter what, but you can control where it goes before then.

Now I'm in this struggle with cancer. I know that I'm not going to win this one at the end of the day, but I am going to do it on my terms as much as possible.

This morning I got up and my body was aching. As my wife Connie said to me, it could just be age. I'm fifty-three now and that doesn't feel the same as twenty-two. Then again, at twenty-two I was a lazy son of a bitch. I still am. I could sleep until four in the afternoon. Anyway, there are pills for the aches, and I take them and they work. I will myself to live longer. I just want to do it.

I am not religious, but I feel I've been tested many times, and I see this cancer as the challenge of challenges.

I am realistic enough to be almost certain I can't win out-right, but I count every day that I keep the cancer at bay as a victory. It's like being in a spaceship being chased by Klingons. How can I stay away from them and find a way to stop every once in a while to turn and take a shot at them? Right now I feel like Kirk calling out, "Scotty, where are my goddamned engines?" They're not here. I'm pragmatic about this. It would be nice if I could beat it. Realistically, it's a longshot. But if I could do it, it would be pretty fuck-ing cool. It would be the ultimate ego-booster, because if I could do this, people would be in awe, which I'd like.

∘━✦━∘

I like to disrupt the usual ways of doing things. I don't accept that there is one way of doing something just because that's the way it's usually done. I like to break things down and build them back again in my way.

That's what I am doing with my cancer, by trying everything in every combination, including going off che-motherapy for an entire month. The risk is that it could all go wrong and in a month from now I'd be gone. Not that it would happen that quickly, but that's how I work in the rest of my life — by doing the unexpected.

I liked to go to business meetings and say, "I need a blowjob." People would be totally flustered. It would catch them off guard so much that they would have to pay atten-tion to whatever I said next. Sometimes you have to do something outlandish like that to get people's attention, and shock them out of their petty distractions and com-fortable silences. It's also pretty fun.

I like to play with life in the same way. Life's too short as it is to get up, work nine to five, come home, take a shit, beg for sex, go to sleep, and get up and do it again. I can't live a routine life. I want to be a slot machine. I like not knowing for sure what's going to happen next. Just pull the handle and maybe I'll win and maybe I won't. That's what life is like for me right now: I have no idea what's around the next corner. Still, I try to influence how it works, especially when it comes to my cancer.

I'm not scared. I am just doing what I want to do in the way I want to do it. It's like it was in my business. I couldn't force people to use my bank machines. I had to have a certain belief that if I put them in the right places and made sure they worked properly, people would use them. Now, with this cancer I have to have a certain belief that if I reject what I have, I can nullify it to a certain extent. I'm not in denial. I know I have it, but as long as I have a choice I'm going to keep living no matter what. I use every weapon I can find to stop it or to slow it, and then I simply push it to the side. I feel it once in a while, and there's no denying that one day I'll have to face it. But I truly believe in what I'm doing. I think that's it. I have no doubt about it at all. I don't need a religious authority or a clairvoyant to tell me I can live an extra two months. This is the middle of 2009. In the worst case, if everything starts to go wrong right now, I'd still get six months. That would get me to Christmas. If I get there or I don't get there, that's fine. I don't think in those terms. Every day I get up and do my thing, enjoy my life and see where the adventure takes me. Since I have had cancer, every day is an adventure for me.

Some days I just sit and watch TV all day. That may sound pretty ordinary, but it's something I have never done since I was a kid watching *Wide World of Sports*. The other day I went golfing with the senior management people at my favourite casino, Fallsview, in Niagara Falls. It was a perfect day for me. I went golfing on the Ussher's Creek course at Legends on the Niagara. The hawks were flying above. I'm not a great golfer, but it was a nice day out, an intimate boys' time. We all came away from that golf game feeling good. That's how I want to leave my life: feeling good, like I've had my day on the golf course. I don't play that hot, but I've had fun.

I'm not sure exactly what form it will take, but I am planning to make a video to be shown at my funeral, one that will show me as I am now, still in control, still looking like myself in the way I want people to think of me.

I know that I wish I had a few minutes of video of the people I've lost, just to say hello. Just so my last memory of them wouldn't be their final days or moments.

I want to share with people that I am glad they have been my friends in my life, that I am a happy person. I especially want it for my children. It's going to be hard for them. It would be hard for me if I was them.

There will still be grieving, but death is not the end of a person. I am already living through my friends, my children, my book, and my movie. I could be in a cubbyhole in an old folks' home, drooling in my underwear and waiting for death to come to me, but I wouldn't have any dignity.

Death is morbid. Too morbid for me. When people die these days, their loved ones often hold a celebration of life afterward. I think that's great. I've had a great life, and my death won't take that away. The main difference will be that you won't be able to talk to me in the way that you used to talk to me. You won't be able to hear me swearing in my usual way.

We had a party at Fallsview when my company hooked up its ten thousandth bank machine. It was just after my diagnosis. We had a great time. We had a band and the Second City comedy troupe. People thought I'd be dead three months later. There were more than two hundred people there, including my staff, my peers, my parents, and my kids. I enjoyed myself, and I'd like to think my funeral will have some of the same feel to it.

If people look at this book I hope they get some hope, they have some laughs, they find some things they can relate to. I don't think of myself as abnormal, though I do and say things that some people wish they could do and say but don't. The point is: everybody can do what I've done and more, if they want to. If you take Mischa Weisz in 1991, who was sitting there in a row house, unemployed, and you take the lady next door who was also unemployed, what made one succeed while the other didn't? The will to live.

Even now with this cancer, I live, enjoy, and hope. I don't feel that much different than I did before I got the cancer. Some people choose to die before they're dead. I choose to live.

I truly like my life, even this way. I could have died of a heart attack and never said anything. I could have died with no closure. It would have been awful not to be able to do the things I have been doing.

I walked into the surgeon's office and I wasn't expecting bad news. When he told me there wasn't anything he could do, and I had four or five months to live, it sounded cold.

He referred me to the Juravinski Cancer Centre and said I'd get in there in about a month. I don't work that way. I wanted to be in there the next week and using some pull and some connections, I got in. You would think as soon as something like that happens, a social worker and other people would get involved, and somebody would help you tell your kids and there would be a counsellor at the school to help them.

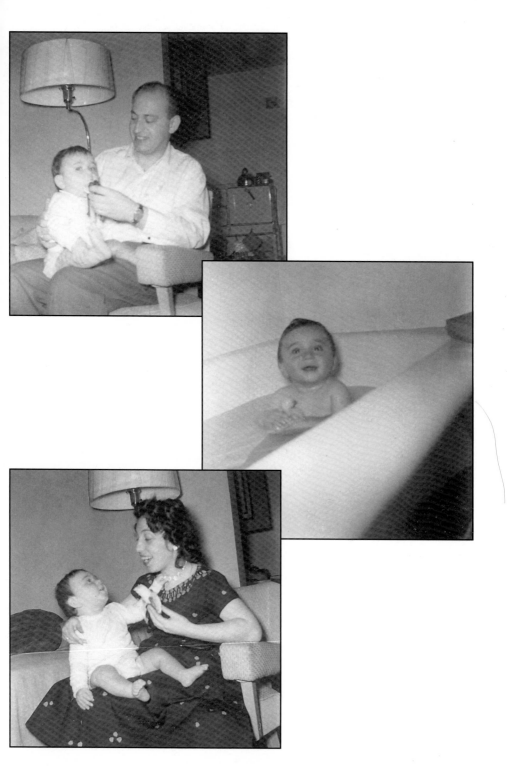

Top: *Baby Mischa with his father, Erich Weisz.* Middle: *Baby Mischa in the bath.*
Bottom: *Baby Mischa with his mother, Emmy Weisz.*

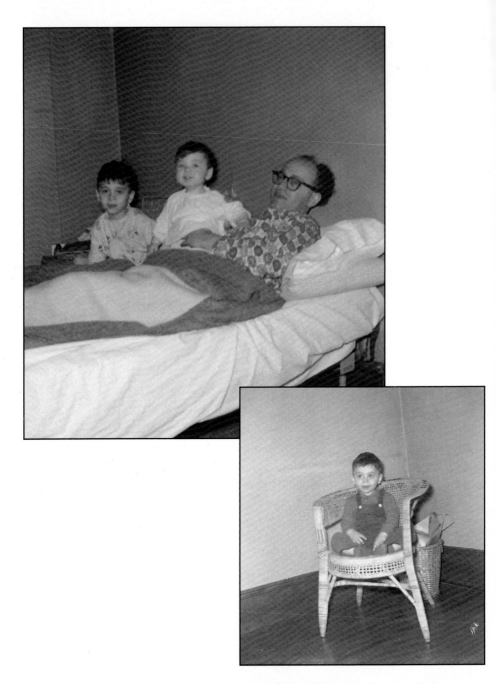

Top: *Mischa with his younger brother, Guido, and their father.* Bottom: *Mischa hangs out.*

Top: *Mischa outside the family home.* Bottom: *Father and son, circa 1973. Mischa was able to grow a beard very early.*

Top: *Mischa about the time he moved out of the family home.* Bottom: *Mischa not long after he started working at the Hamilton Wentworth Credit Union.*

Top: *Mischa and his first wife, Marcella.* Bottom: *Guido Weisz and his wife, Bonnie.*

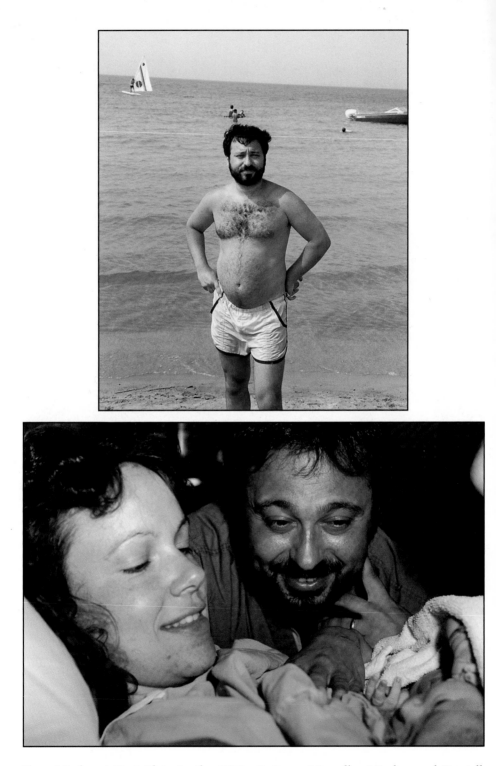

Top: *Mischa at Port Elgin in the 1980s.* Bottom: *Marcella, Mischa, and Danielle, shortly after Danielle's birth.*

Top: *Baby Nathan*. Bottom left: *Baby Danielle*. Bottom right: *Nathan and Danielle at Lake Ontario.*

Top: *Nathan and Danielle at Christmas.* Bottom: *Nathan as a boy.*

CHAPTER 2
Unanswered Questions

I grew up in my parents' home, and I know they worked hard to make a nice life for us. But they did not include me in their world, and that shaped the person I became.

I didn't even know what my background was until some kids at school called me a Jew, and I went to my parents to ask what that meant. They told me I was Jewish, and that was all. I was maybe thirteen at the time, and it meant nothing to me. What the kids had said hadn't hurt my feelings, because it didn't mean anything to me. It had simply confused me.

Until then, I had never considered my identity in any particular religious or cultural context other than broadly considering myself to be of European background, and I still don't talk much about it today.

I have celebrated Christmas my whole life, in a secular way. I am simply not a religious person.

You know what we used to put on our Christmas tree? Sausages. What a way to die! Get up Christmas morning, unwrap the sausages, and eat them, one after another. It was funny as hell. We always had a Christmas tree. You would think if we were of a different religion, we wouldn't have had a Christmas tree, but we had one every year. I think my parents might have been compensating because they thought it would be safer if their children could blend into society, but it left me in a strange position.

Today, when people ask me, "Are you Jewish?" I say, "Yes I've got Jewish blood in me, but I don't practice." I've never even been in a synagogue.

Did I have a *Leave It to Beaver* family? No. Does everybody wish they had that family? Sure they do. I'm afraid that in some critical ways my parents are very strange to me, very foreign. I never got real access to what drove them, because I feel they were shielding me from it. As a result, I don't understand their values, their concepts. I'm a right wing, capitalist son of a gun, and they're left wing, save the world types. In that regard, we don't see eye to eye on much of anything. Do I love my parents? Yes I do. But do I like my parents? I don't understand them, so I don't know how to like them in a straightforward way.

Part of the reason I don't understand them is that I don't really know them. I know they are Holocaust survivors. My father, Erich, came from Austria. My mother, Emmy, came from Holland.

Some of my mother's relatives are alive, and some of them perished during the war. Most of my father's family perished in the war. That's as much as I know. I think my father was in a camp, and my mother was in hiding, though I can't say I know even that much for certain.

I simply don't know a lot about my family or my background; very little. I am not sure why, but they have never offered to share it with me, and after fifty-three years of my life, that has created a gap we can't bridge.

I came to resent it in a way. They may have been of a certain race, a certain religion, but I didn't even know what I was until I was a teenager. I went to the Unitarian church next to our house and nobody at home ever told me I was Jewish. It's like somebody saying to you, "Gee, your mother isn't your mother, you're somebody else's."

Once I knew it, just never sat with me right. I could never embrace it, never understand it, and I don't know where to place it. To this day, I don't get into conversations when people ask, "Where are you from?" In a way, when someone asks me that, I want to punch the person out for prying into my personal background. I don't talk about that shit. People ask me, "Why don't you ever ask questions like that?" It's none of my business. It's fine with me if somebody wants to say, "Hey, I'm from Hungary." But I don't pry, ever.

When it comes to the war, my parents talk around it, but they don't talk about it. I find that they live in their past, and they only live there privately. Maybe that's a disease that comes from war, or maybe it's their way of maintaining a separation between the chapters of their lives, but I don't know how to understand it or appreciate it. If I could, I would help them get past it so they could start living and enjoying their family, and enjoying the things around them. Instead, it seems to me like they're living in 1942, all by themselves. They're not open about it, and after so much time I just don't ask, so it's a complete mystery to me. That puts a distance between us. For whatever reason, they're insular, and that puts a block between the generations.

I do know my parents came to Canada in 1954. I know they went to British Columbia for a time because my father's sister was living there.

I was born in Barrie, Ontario, on March 8, 1956. My father was in the Canadian Army at that time, at Camp Borden, in the musical section. We then moved southwest to St. Thomas, Ontario, where my brother, Guido, was born February 2, 1959. My father had become a music teacher, and that's where he started his profession. Shortly after that we moved to Don Mills and then to Ancaster Heights, on the edge of Hamilton, in 1961.

When I was young we spoke Dutch at home. I don't remember it at all now, though when I hear it my tongue goes all funny and I want to speak that way again. Later, when Guido and I were a little older, our parents would speak to one another in Dutch when they didn't want us to know what they were saying. I maintained at least enough of a grasp to realize when I was in shit.

Guido and I tried to make up our own private language, which we called Martian, but even that ended up sounding pretty much like Dutch.

Right from the start, school and I weren't friends, and grammar, spelling, and sometimes even pronunciation are still weak points for me. Even after I learned English, I had to go for speech therapy because I didn't pronounce certain words correctly, like "spaghetti" or "chrysanthemum," and there are certain words I still can't pronounce properly to this day.

I was a lazy student with a short attention span, and I'm sure my health issues didn't help much. I had irritable bowel syndrome and I was asthmatic. I used to spend a lot of time in the hospital as a kid. I remember one of my stays in the hospital when I was about five years old. Back then, they didn't have oxygen masks, they had oxygen tents. I remember when the nurse came with my breakfast one morning. It was a boiled egg and toast, and it was outside the barrier and I couldn't get it. I remember staring at it because there was nobody there to help me. I remember her coming back and asking, "You're not hungry?" and I thought, "How do I get my egg?" It's the strangest memory, but I often think back on it: how do I get that egg? Maybe that was the challenge that started my drive to succeed.

We moved a couple more times in the same area of the city before my family moved down to Aberdeen Avenue, in the southwestern part of the old city, a nice neighbourhood just below the escarpment. It was a pretty big house. My parents each had their own bathroom on the second floor and my dad had a separate study to teach private music lessons. Guido and I had our bedrooms on the third floor.

We had moved in next door to a family called the Helts. One of my best friends to this day, Frank Helt, is part of that family, and later, another person who was destined to become one of my lifelong friends, Paul Buckle, would move in farther down the same street.

Despite the emotional distance between our parents and us, we still knew they loved us because they worked hard to make sure we had a comfortable life. My mom would make European style roasts and other dishes. I remember when she used to serve beef tongue. It tasted good, but looked so weird.

We travelled quite a bit. We took nice vacations, though they were more adult style, cultural vacations than the kind that my friends took with their families. We'd go to Europe to look at architecture, not to Disneyland to play. Still, we enjoyed ourselves on those vacations, and I have nice memories, such as flying kites in Holland with my father.

My parents did a lot for Guido and me on our birthdays and Christmas, and those were good times, too. We always had nice presents and good food. On special occasions, like birthdays, my parents always got a marzipan cake from a European deli downtown. I would have my friends over for birthday parties when I was smaller, but that fell off when I got older, and the atmosphere at home seemed unwelcoming to noise and play. It was serious and formal and somewhat tense, and I stopped having friends over.

My parents are intellectuals and they acted that way even around us. That was the opposite of what I wanted as a child. When they got together with people their own age, once in a while they might have a couple glasses of wine and I would see them let their hair down, but I wished they would be more open and tender with me.

My parents weren't big sports fans, so I didn't grow up playing hockey and baseball like a lot of kids from more established Canadian families. My parents worked. That's basically what they did. They were always busy. My mom did a lot of volunteer work and spent a lot of time studying to become a social worker. She was in her forties when she got her degree.

On top of teaching music in Hamilton's public high schools, my father was giving private lessons after school and on weekends, so my interaction with my parents wasn't a lot. I depended on myself. My parents and I did some day-to-day things together, but not many. They were workaholics as far as I'm concerned. Maybe they needed to work that hard to give us a nice lifestyle, or maybe they needed to do it to assure themselves they would be secure, but I know I would have liked more of their time and fewer of their barriers.

As kids, Guido and I played together a lot. I remember doing the usual mean big brother things, like holding him down so the dog would lick him all over. What's weird is that I honestly don't remember many details from when my brother and I were kids, and for some reason, neither does he. I don't know why. I know I spent a tremendous amount of time in my room working on electronics while my brother was across the hallway in his room.

We went away to summer camps quite a bit, but because we were three years apart we ended up staying with different groups. Once, on a long trip to Europe, our parents sent us to a camp in the Netherlands, where the counsellors and campers could barely speak any English and we could barely speak any Dutch. That was difficult. A place we enjoyed much better was Unicamp, operated by the Unitarian Church much closer to home in Orangeville, Ontario, which was pretty lighthearted compared to some of the other places we had been.

I was the first person in my group to start growing whiskers and one summer at Unicamp, I grew a scruffy beard without Guido knowing. On the day our parents were coming to get us, he ran right past me without recognizing me, and I broke into a big smile when he came back and did a double take.

My brother and I grew up to be very different people. He's more of a detail guy than I am, and his political ideas lie closer to our parents' than mine. But we are still close. We are like those friends who you don't necessarily talk to every day, or even every week, but when you do talk you catch up easily and it's like no time has passed. My brother lives in Ottawa, where he's really passionate about his government job. His wife, Bonnie, lives in Victoria. They bought some property there, and eventually they want to build there. When they were out there, the job she really wanted with the provincial government in British Columbia came open, so she's living there now until they can be together.

My daughter Danielle lives in Victoria, too, just three minutes from where Bonnie lives. That's very comforting to me, because if something happens to me, Bonnie can scoop up Danielle and get her here. After I go, it means Danielle will have someone to console her and help her.

○━┼━○

When I was a kid I learned to play the piano and the flute. I remember going downtown to the Hamilton Conservatory of Music for my piano lessons. I would take the bus for ten cents and go to the farmers' market afterward. Downtown Hamilton was full of character and full of characters then.

My father bought me a flute and gave me lessons for a couple of years, starting when I was about twelve. He had a reputation as a good, very disciplined teacher, both in the high schools and as a private instructor. When he wasn't teaching, my dad was always practising the piano and the flute. The house was full of music, but there didn't appear to be a lot of emotion flowing from it. I think the emotion was probably there, but it was all turned inward.

When it was time for my lessons, my father treated me just like any other student. He had me to his study and he gave me my lesson once a week. He taught me scales and theory and classical music, in addition to what I was learning on piano at the conservatory.

I looked forward to the lessons in the beginning, but by the end I had come to dread them. He was doing his best and I was doing my best, but I felt like I could never be good enough for him. I tried and I tried, but by the end I just didn't want to do it any more.

One thing I've learned is that no matter what, you need praise — in your family, at school, at work. I may be very critical, but I do believe in praise.

I went to the public elementary and middle schools in our neighbourhood, Earl Kitchener and Ryerson, before going on to Westdale Secondary School.

Westdale was great for me personally, but did not inspire me scholastically. I did what I needed to do to pass, but no more. I skipped a lot of classes, or got permission to go to the washroom and never returned. Academically, they thought I was a dummy. They were going to send me to vocational school, but then they found that I was bright, just lazy, and had an attitude problem. Attitude's been a problem with me all my life, I think.

It's just that if something is being taught and I don't see the practical purpose for it, then why would I want to learn it? Take calculus, for example. I started to learn it, but then I'd wonder, "What the fuck am I going to use this for?" I got bored.

That kind of thinking didn't go over well at home, either. My parents wanted me to focus on my education. Their belief was that if you don't have a good education, you don't become anything, and the distance between us grew.

A bright spot in high school was being selected as one of two grade eleven students to go to McMaster University, about a mile away from Westdale, to learn computer science.

But I got bored there, too, and instead of doing the project I was supposed to do, I fooled around and used the computer to make Snoopy cartoon calendars. That was the early 1970s, and back then we had to do everything on computer cards. Every Saturday and Sunday, I went to McMaster and made boxes and boxes of those cards to do it. The staff got mad because I was misusing the printer, but I thought it was great. It was a great challenge and it was fun, even if they didn't think so. I kept those cards for years.

I did enjoy the social side of high school, especially the extracurricular activities. I was on the nerdy side, so I was in the chess club and the boosters club.

Most of all, I loved acting. I was in school productions and I really enjoyed that. I got so confident that one summer I applied at the Stratford Festival, but they turned me down flat. I was crushed and defeated. I'm not good with rejection at all.

I do know that acting helped me to become a great salesperson. Unlike calculus, it did come in handy in other parts of life.

My friend Frank said to me once, "I'm good-looking. I'm tall. I could sit at a bar all night and not one woman would approach me. You're short, you're fat, and you're rude, but women will come up to you all night."

I said, "You know why? Because I've got charisma, and that brings a lot to the table."

I make a lot of eye contact with people. I learned that from acting. You know the movie *Alfie*? I watched an interview with the guy who played the original Alfie, Michael Caine. He was talking about acting, and one of the things he said has stayed with me ever since: when you see actors on the screen, they never blink. They stare intensely all the time, and it commands a lot of attention. When I talk to people I do the same thing, because I like to be in control of the conversation. I like to be in control in general. That's who I am. I like to make sure my point gets across.

I really wanted to have more of a social life in high school, but my parents were very strict, so I had to be home by nine o'clock, eleven on Saturdays. I still remember having to leave a girlfriend at a concert one Saturday night because I had to be home by eleven o'clock. I was not a happy camper at that time.

My parents were very old-fashioned in the way they raised us: protective, formal and focused on discipline. If you got out of line, you felt the wrath. My father was a very strict European type. He sat at the table and commanded that you not speak until you were spoken to. No one was to start eating until our mother sat down, even if it was twenty-five minutes later after she finished scurrying around.

Was it normal? Was it not normal? I don't know. What I know is that I spent a lot of time on my own, reading science fiction. That and electronics were my passions. I dabbled in ham radios and CB radios. Those are the hobbies that kept me going. As I said, I was a bit of a nerd. When I was in my room by myself I would build things with my soldering iron. I tried to build an electronic keyboard as a project.

My parents worked most of the time, so we were on our own a lot, even when they were working at home. We weren't allowed to have many friends over, and I wouldn't really have wanted to anyway. It wasn't a place to hang out. I was supposed to be in my room, quiet, at night. Because my father taught music at home, there was to be no noise. It was very solemn, and that drove me crazy.

By the time I reached seventeen, I was determined to get out of the house as soon as I could. I went to work at a Radio Shack store in downtown Hamilton, at King Street East and Mary Street, near the police station. I remember all the cops coming in and buying novelty helmets with flashing red lights. I had a great boss there who taught me a lot about business and life.

I enjoyed Radio Shack because I liked what they sold, and I liked selling. It came naturally to me. If something was sitting there on the sales floor, I liked getting a customer to buy it, even if he didn't want it. It was just something I enjoyed.

I was busting to get out of the house by then. I needed my freedom. I needed to date. My parents' traditions and values did not mix with how I wanted to live at that time, and I have never been one to conform to anything I don't agree with. For me, it was a choice of going completely insane or getting out of the house. I needed a social life. I had to get out and feel like I was part of the crew. I was tired of feeling like an outsider because of all the restrictions.

Today, I love my parents very much, but I still can't say we understand each other in the way I wish we did.

There's a thing called a cancer marker. It's a way of measuring the activity of a cancer. They measure differently for different cancers, including pancreatic cancer, where they measure something called CA-19.

Once a month I go and get a reading. You can only get the test once a month. The cancer marker shows you where you cancer is, and there are trends of it going up, then down and up again. If it goes down, you're happy, which it did for me when I started chemo. It went from 328 to nine, and then eventually it began to creep back up. Now it's just had a big increase, from one hundred to 160. It's scary shit, because you know that guillotine is getting closer.

CHAPTER 3
On My Own

Somehow I finished high school, and when I was eighteen I finally moved out.

I can't remember why, but I took my boxes and boxes of old computer cards with me when I moved into a bachelor apartment in a high-rise on the edge of downtown Hamilton. In reality, it was only about a mile away from my parents' house, but it might as well have been another country as far as I was concerned.

I stacked up those boxes of computer cards inside my apartment and used them as a backstop for my targets so that I could shoot a BB gun in there. It was pretty screwed up, I know. Home had been a strict environment, and I was cutting loose.

I was living on almost nothing when I moved out of the house. I took my mattress and that was about it. I had those air chairs that you blew up. I had about thirty pillows I bought at Woolco downtown. My friends used to take food from their parents' freezers to give to me. Since I was the first among us to move out of the house, my place became the social hangout. My friends would often borrow my key when I left the apartment.

We certainly stirred up our share of trouble. My friends used to put detergent in the fountain in the lobby. The worst thing I ever did was throw a roast I had overcooked into the swimming pool.

After about a year, I moved to a place that was a few blocks down and around the corner, on Queen Street South, a slightly larger apartment in another high-rise. I lived on the tenth floor. I was eighteen or nineteen years old, and I was bad. I had a girlfriend who was fifteen. I was bad, but I was learning.

I knew I needed to survive and I had to figure out a way to do it. My character was developing, based on my experiences. I made tons of mistakes. Tons. But I learned from those mistakes. Could I run for president today and have CNN not do five billion stories on me? No way. There's enough there to keep them going for a lifetime.

But those little things that happened to me as a teenager and in my early twenties made me who I am. They made me stronger and more secure, and helped me catch up on the parts of life that I had missed in high school.

We had a good gang of friends then. From that group two in particular remain my friends: Frank Helt and Paul Buckle.

Frank and I used to go camping at MacGregor Point Provincial Park on Lake Huron, near Port Elgin. We'd go on our own or with his girlfriend, and later wife, Linda, or with Paul and his wife Jackie, and we had our share of adventures.

We were camping once at MacGregor Point when we were in our twenties and something really funny happened. I was with my girlfriend of the time and Frank was with Linda. We'd been smoking pot a little earlier, and a park staffer approached our fire, very earnestly. Later, I jokingly called him Ranger Bob, but we were a little paranoid when we saw him coming up to us.

Ranger Bob came up and said, "We're having a movie night tonight. We're showing a film on insects."

For whatever reason, I didn't hear it that way. I heard "insects" as "incest," and when I asked him about why they were showing a film on incest, Frank and I totally lost it. Ranger Bob didn't have a clue what we were laughing about. It went on for a while, and eventually we recovered and Ranger Bob went on his way. Needless to say, we didn't go to see the insect film that night.

Another time, Frank and I went camping at a KOA campground in Florida, when we caught a piece of a hurricane. He had a small nylon tent, and I had a big old canvas tent. The rain just kept coming into my tent, through the ceiling and walls, and from the ground. It was an incredible storm. I had my sleeping bag on an air mattress and there was so much water that my bed was actually floating inside the tent. Eventually, I had to go sleep in the car. The water was up to the bumper by then.

Frank had a nice little red Opel GT back in those days, and he was very proud of it. Once we were in Port Elgin at a french fry stand. I threw fries at the Opel so the seagulls would go after them and mess up his beautiful car, just to piss him off. But once they realized where the fries were coming from, they came after me instead, and the joke ended up being on me.

My friends are very important to me. I have always enjoyed having conversations with Paul. We've known each other a long time, and we have our own banter. He's an intelligent guy, and we can ramble on and challenge each other and it's interesting. That, and we both have a sick sense of humour.

Frank and I talk almost every day, sometimes for thirty seconds or less, but we talk at least once a day — more often these days because I'm on my way out. Frank is so genuine. He works on my eulogy on his BlackBerry. He hates having to think about it, but he's always working on it because he wants it to be as good as it can be, and that is very touching to me.

When I first moved out, I still had my job at Radio Shack. What a great job. I would ride down to the store on my bicycle and work there, when I wasn't taking classes part-time at Mohawk College. First, I screwed around for half a year, studying business. I didn't like that. Next, I tried electronic technology and I didn't like that either. I never finished a diploma.

I got out of college, quit Radio Shack, and went to work at the Hamilton Wentworth Credit Union. I wanted to have a real job, pay my rent, and be independent. I worked there fifteen years, until 1991.

Over the years, I kept going to school in bits and pieces. I did part of my BA in political science at McMaster. I quit that because I had a professor whose accent I couldn't understand. At least I stayed long enough to learn something important: how the key to power was to mystify the masses.

I studied a little accounting, but it wasn't to my liking either. Eventually, I started to feel the same way I had felt in high school: they don't teach you the right stuff. I had to learn it on my own, through experience.

People with PhDs, MBAs, and so on, I think they're very intelligent in their subjects, but they can be very narrow in their thinking and once you get outside their topics, they're not always that bright. They focus so long on their particular topics that they don't get everything else.

I don't like to learn a whole bunch of one thing. I prefer to learn a little of everything.

◦━━◆━━◦

At the credit union I was such a dick that everybody moved me all the time. I'm not confrontational so much as I don't like politics. I don't like bullshit. I don't like drama. I just want to get the job done.

I was a loans manager, mortgage manager, branch manager. I went into data management, and then I became systems manager, taking care of the computer stuff. But of all the areas I worked in there, the collections department was probably the most interesting.

I was there three years, and that's where I got to see the evil side of humanity: how much they would lie and cheat and sneak to try to get out of their obligations. Unfortunately,

I ruined a lot of people's lives by collecting things. I even collected a motorcycle from a bike gang member. I had no fear. I don't know why, but I never did.

I would start the day with a number of files and start phoning delinquents. "Ring! Ring! Hi. You're $27.56 behind in last month's payments. What do you plan to do about it?"

I would call people and try to do refinancing if I could, but people were lying ninety-eight percent of the time. Eventually there would be foreclosures and repossessions. For the first six months I would ask, "When are you going to make your payment?" They'd say, "I'm going to make it on Thursday," or whatever, but when the day came, hardly any of them paid. By sheer experience I learned that people, especially in a time of crisis, don't necessarily do what they say they're going to do.

My time in collections was one of those periods when working became interesting for me, because people would sit down and I would just wait to see how much bullshit they were going to try to throw at me before they really started to show the cracks. It got to the point where I would say, "I don't really think you're going to pay on the thirtieth, so here's what's going to happen: we're going to take your car." Or your house, or whatever.

Then we'd start getting somewhere.

Only when you really threaten someone's welfare do they really react. Until then, they don't believe anything is going to happen.

I enjoyed the job. It made me a little more cynical about people, but I also learned that with many problems, the best way is to blow up the situation, so that you can put it back together your way. The best dynamite for that is often shock.

Back then lending money was different. It was the three Cs: collateral, character, and capacity. It basically came down to a judgment call. Sometimes I would say, "There's no way that that person should have a loan," and I would be overridden or get a lot of shit for it, and they would get the loan and go bankrupt three months later.

Don't get me wrong. I love people. I really do. I like to understand how people interact. Because of my experience, I can spend twenty seconds with a person and figure them out. Collections, Radio Shack, anyplace where I've had to deal with people, I've loved it, because it was a chance to find out more about people and how to deal with them. I wasn't a saint. I was an asshole sometimes, because I didn't know any different. But if you get told enough times that you can't be that way, then you change your approach. That's what made me a better person. The more I got to interact with people, the better I understood them and the better I could interrelate with them.

Did I feel bad in collections? After five people, yes. After ten, maybe, but after a little while longer, not that much. You get to learn that most people bring it on themselves. There were some people I felt bad for, who had been through something terrible that was beyond their control: their husband died, or their wife left them. But most people do it to themselves, and I didn't feel as bad for them.

Some people have ten credit cards, for example. More than thirty years later I still see it at the casino all the time. It's amazing. They use them for cash advances. They open up their wallets and you see them. If each one is worth

$10,000 or $15,000, they can get themselves into $100,000 or $150,000 debt. That reminds me so much of my collection days. I can see the problems coming.

Collections just became my job. I can distance myself very quickly from a situation that might emotionally fuck me up, and that certainly was one that could do it to me. I hate drama. I don't want it. I learned just to do my job.

Now, I never get stressed out about that kind of shit. I have learned from the occasions where I have been stressed out that it isn't worth it. It doesn't get you anywhere. I don't want to say I'm a Vulcan or anything, but I have learned it just doesn't get me anything. It wastes time and energy. I remember once in my later years there, when I was in systems management and we were converting the credit union to an in-house computer system. We had to get some ATMs, and there was a problem getting them on-line. I was devastated. I remember spending the day feeling like I wanted to kill myself. After a couple of hours, I thought, "This is stupid. There was nothing I could do and it wasn't my fault."

Now when something is stressful, I say, "This is what I need to do. This is how I learn. This is how I grow."

That was a very important lesson for me: I was starting to learn how to take a problem and depersonalize it. Once you take the emotion out of a problem — even one you really care about — it becomes much, much easier to resolve. Unfortunately, I didn't learn it quite well enough to avoid getting pulled through the knothole in my personal life. But there are lessons everywhere.

Collections was where I met my first wife, Marcella. She sat across from me. She was more of a clerk and I was more of a manager when we started to date. It was going really well, I thought, and we were ready to take the next step, so I thought I would propose.

She opened her desk and found her engagement ring in the drawer. That's where I asked her to marry me, right there in the office. That wasn't too romantic of me. I look back on some of the things I've done and ask myself, "What the fuck were you thinking?"

I like my doctors and I trust them. I have taken a different approach by using Western medical treatment while also trying everything else that won't interfere with what they're doing, including traditional Chinese medicine, following a special diet, and taking supplements. I have even hired a consultant to analyze my cancer at the molecular level.

When you keep hearing, "I don't know what to do for you," you've got to take matters into your own hands.

My blood sugar was running high a few weeks ago — about double the level where they declare you to be diabetic. I told that to my Chinese doctor. He changed the formula of my tea and my sugar level dropped like a stone. It's so funny. There's Western medicine, there's Eastern medicine, and they seem to be helping each other.

CHAPTER 4
Marriage, Family, Parting

Marcella was a stunning woman, who had outer and inner beauty, and a sweetness that really drew me to her. I was very much in love with her when we were first married.

Our first date was actually the outcome of a bet with my colleagues, who had pushed me to see if I could date her. She was engaged to someone else at the time, and preparing to get married.

Someone at the office said, "Wow, look at that beauty."

I said, "I can date her in ten days or less."

The bet was on.

Sure, I wanted to win, but what drove me was that I really wanted to be with her. I asked her if she would like to go out on a date and she said no, but then a couple of days later she called and said she had changed her mind. I don't know what it is exactly, but I have a way that can be very charming and convincing. Once we went out, it took off very quickly.

We had only been dating three months by the time we got engaged. Like me, Marcella is the child of immigrant parents. She is brown-eyed and beautiful, and fulfilled my youthful, sentimental vision of the ideal wife and mother.

We got married in a Catholic church because she is Catholic. I went to marriage classes and the whole bit. I knew the Catholic wedding made my parents a little squeamish, but I was in love and I wanted to do it the way Marcella wanted to do it. We got married May 28, 1982, at 6:30 p.m., with about 150 or two hundred people there. I had really wanted to get married and have a family, and I was pleased with the way it was turning out. I was very sentimental and I still am.

I was very happy that this part of my life had come together. Unfortunately, I hadn't known — or at least admitted to myself — that we weren't really ready for it. Both of us still had growing up to do, but I was simply happy and unable to see beyond that.

There were many good times in our marriage, and at first we were able to overcome the difficulties that began to emerge. Although we sometimes argued and hurt one another with the things we said and did, we got along very well most of the time. We enjoyed each other and tried to work on having children. We had trouble conceiving, so we went to fertility clinics and tried a lot of things through the early years of our marriage, in an effort to have kids.

Sadly, our marriage was nearly over by the time we finally reached that goal.

Over the years, the arguing and conflict in our marriage was finally starting to smother the love that had brought us together. It didn't happen all at once, and the inevitable conclusion wasn't as obvious at the time as it would be afterward.

We'd have really good times and then we'd have really shitty times. There were gaps of several months between our arguments sometimes, when we'd have good times and talk about having kids. You always think that if you get pregnant, things will get better.

Marcella and I were married for nine years of ups and downs, and the kids came at the tail end, just as the last of the love that had sustained us was draining away.

Danielle Alexandra was born in 1988, in the eighteenth minute, of the eighteenth hour, of the eighteenth day, of the eighth month. It was really bizarre. She came out with her cord around her neck, but there was no damage.

Nathan Michael was born August 11, 1990. He was in breech position, so I got to see him bum first. I got to cut his cord.

We had two healthy kids, and we loved them with all our hearts, but it didn't do anything to solve the problems that Marcella and I were having. We separated, and started a long court battle over who should have the kids. It was awful and draining and painful for all of us.

Nathan was still a baby when we first separated. Danielle was a toddler. She was so cute. She was very precocious, very outspoken. If I ever took the video camera out to take a video of Nathan, I could count on Danielle getting herself in front of the lens. She always wanted the attention. She's always had a mind of her own and has always been a big talker. I think her outspokenness of today started when she was a baby. When she cried, it sent shivers down your spine. It was one of those cries you could hear anywhere in the world.

After my wife and I first separated, I lived for the first six months on the sofa down in the basement. One of the few bright spots of those days for me was that every morning at 6:00, Danielle would come down and snuggle up with me on the couch. That was great. We spent a lot of time together that way.

I had an interesting choice to make around that time. I could have gone the normal route and said, "Okay, take the kids," and gone on and gotten married again and had more kids, but I found it very important to take care of my children. I wanted the children. Most men didn't do that back then. It was very rare. But that's what I wanted, and that's what I worked for.

It looked like I was going to lose at one point because I didn't have another woman, and by then Marcella had a boyfriend, creating what was considered a more suitable environment. At first we shared custody of the kids. I challenged it, arguing that I should be the custodial parent. She basically ran out of money, and said I could take the kids. They were preschoolers then and I have taken care of them ever since.

The whole process was really awful, and I spent a lot of time in counselling. I was screwed up. I didn't know what to do. I was doing something very nontraditional. A male fighting for his kids wasn't normal. A man would usually walk away, find somebody else and start over again.

Today, Marcella and I are on friendly terms. She has been understanding and sympathetic through my illness, and has helped our kids through these hard times. I know she still cares about me, and I do wish her well.

In the middle of my marriage falling apart, my job at the Hamilton Wentworth Credit Union was declared redundant and I was let go.

I got a contract at the Ontario Civil Servants Credit Union in Toronto, a job that ended around the time I was getting custody of the kids. I didn't bother going to get another job, because I knew I was going to have my hands full. I was down, financially — no money and looking after the kids. I was living on unemployment insurance. I didn't mind much, though, because I had my children. We sold the family house and Marcella and I split the proceeds. I went to live with the kids in a subsidized townhouse along the edge of what today is the Lincoln Alexander Parkway, on Hamilton Mountain. I loved looking after them, and although money was tight, I look back on that as a golden period in my life. It was also a period of my life when I learned a lot about myself. Through the challenges of being a single dad and living in social housing, I became determined to make the most of my life, and to make the best life possible for my kids.

Later, when I was doing better financially, I would take the kids to Disney World and I loved it. When I go back there now, as I still do, I see those characters that my kids used to run up to, and it stirs up very, very warm feelings for me. I remember the things we did and the things they said as kids, and it makes me think about how quickly the time has passed. But I know they are going to remember those things, and that makes me profoundly happy. I showed my kids a lot more of myself than my parents had done with me, and it made me feel great. I worked hard to be able to raise Danielle and Nathan, and I know it was well worth the fight.

If I have any advice for people now it's that no matter what situation you get into, learn to pause for a few seconds before you say or do anything, and just bring yourself to a certain level of calm. People react, sometimes very crazily, to things — especially in relationships when they're so close to the trees that they can't see the forest. Both of us did it. I learned that being mad or irrational doesn't get you anywhere. It gets you no solution. You have to pause and ask, "What's the solution here? What can I do better?" Don't expect other people to fix things for you. You have to fix them for yourself, or else avoid them. Any problem is fixable, to a point.

But you can't change people. I learned that by experience. The art of a good relationship is to be able to negotiate between the two of you. If you have a problem, you have to be able to work out a resolution reasonably. Sometimes, though, you never do. You can't expect to have a solution for every problem in your life. There are problems in life sometimes for which there are no solutions. If you were my wife and you picked your nose every time you watched TV and I said, "That's disgusting," but you just couldn't help it, I would have to live with it and just hand you a Kleenex. Some things you just can't change.

I have told my kids that the hardest thing they're going to have to work on in their lives is a relationship. It's work. It's psychological, because you're dealing with a person who is not you, and they're going to change over time, just like you will. You'll think you know them, but you never really will. They'll surprise you sometimes, and you'll surprise them. But it's important not to change yourself for somebody else. Ever. As soon as you change the essence of who you are, you're not you any more and you won't like yourself any more.

Any experience I've had in life and work, outside raising my kids, has removed me farther from dealing with things by using my feelings. I now take problems and put them outside myself and look at them there. Is it a good thing? Is it a bad thing? I don't know. It makes me more objective about things, but it makes me less emotional. It's not that I'm without emotion. I still cry in a movie. If it moves me, tears will be streaming down my face. It's just that in serious, real life situations, I stop and ask myself what I am about to sacrifice by becoming emotional, and at what cost?

You know what it is? I think it relates back to my work in collections, but when people have a problem and they tell me they can't do anything, or won't, it pisses me off. You know what? They can do something.

I've raised two children, because I can. I've built companies, because I can. I'm fighting my cancer, because I can. When people say they can't, or won't, or don't, it pisses me off. It's annoying.

I'm a realistic optimist. I know that shit happens. To me, everything in life has to be balanced. There has got to be balance in life. If you came to me with a problem I would listen to it and objectively say, "This is what I think." I wouldn't care if I hurt your feelings at all. I would just state the facts of the situation as I saw them. I care about people. I respect people who are willing to face their problems and fix their problems. That's a thrill.

I've had fifty-four chemos. I am basically living on chemo three weeks out of each month. I like to be in control. I like to be in control of myself in my situation. I think I have good control even right now, today. It bothers me that I cannot control this cancer. I know that's stupid. I'm smart enough to know that shit happens, but I have to have a belief that this can be conquered. You have to do something. If you do nothing, nothing will happen. If you do something, maybe something will happen.

I go see a lady who does this work using the power of the mind to rid me of this cancer. It's a little hocus-pocus, I know, but I do it because I don't know it doesn't work. People tell me my credibility is shot because I go to a voodoo person, but even if it helps me to believe a little more strongly, why not?

CHAPTER 5
A New Start

On the last day before she left the company, my secretary told me she still didn't know me. She'd been with me seven years, and she said every time she thought she was getting to know me, I would change. I don't feel myself change, but I consider what she said to be a tremendous compliment. If you don't change, especially in business, it's all over. I have always tried to be as flexible and as decisive as possible.

If I follow a course, and it doesn't seem like it's working I'll say, "Let's go right, let's go left." Nobody else understands why, but I do, and to me that's all that matters.

I think that adapting to change is a big part of why I was able to find so much success operating around the perimeter of the big banks.

I think of the big banks as being like aircraft carriers filled with thousands of MBAs. If the captain orders the crew to tack, the first MBA wonders, "What does he really mean? Is it best?" And on it goes, until the time you get to the five thousandth MBA and you're hundreds of miles downstream, still going straight ahead. The way I have learned to run my businesses and my life is to take action quickly. If I want to tack, I tack, and it's done. I have learned to be resilient. You have got to work with things changing in the business world and in the personal world.

I can teach you the mechanics of a bicycle. I can show you how all the gears work, how the tires stay inflated, and how everything interrelates. But unless you get on the bicycle, you actually have no fucking clue how it really works. That's the trouble with MBAs. It's all hypothetical. And not only that, it's their own particular idea of the hypothetical. They talk about reports. I say screw the reports. What does your gut tell you? When you ask an MBA that, they can't respond, because they've never been taught to think with their gut. You know on *Star Trek* when Captain Kirk asks Spock, "What does your gut tell you, Spock?" and Spock answers, "We don't think that way." Well Spock is your MBA. Kirk is your entrepreneur. That's the trouble with MBAs. They don't know how to get emotionally involved in business.

With business, I love the process of the game. I never imagined I'd end up with thirteen thousand ATMs. It was just like getting on that little sailboat, and seeing where we could go. As it went along there were opportunities, and there were challenges. We stopped and picked up the opportunities, and we sailed around or through the challenges and fixed the damage when we needed to. Sometimes it was more work, and different work than I would have thought, and sometimes we had to go a little farther than I would have imagined, but we got there.

Running a business means knowing how to see the trends and adjust to them — in sales, in cash flow, and transactions — and keeping everything upright and moving forward, while anticipating what's going to happen next. It's just part of my nature that I can understand the life of a business.

Look at the economy. The trouble with the automakers was that they never changed. They were arrogant. They stayed the same. They stayed the course. This whole recession we're in is not really a recession, it's a correction of MBAs and unions. Both were taking out too much money and not seeing the changes that were happening in other countries. This is a correction of that.

I like running businesses. I went to school at night and I got my credit union certification. I got most of my accountancy certification, but I never finished it.

I learned enough about political science to know you have to mystify the masses. Make sure the customer thinks he is buying what he needs. It's all in the presentation. You can bullshit your whole life through.

By the time I got into business for myself, I had all the skills I needed. I had my sales training from Radio Shack. I had my corporate bullshit training from the credit union days. I had my technology training from the credit union, too, and after a few years on the consulting side, I had learned to analyze problems and find solutions very quickly.

I have had my failures, for sure, in business and in life. I don't like failure, but I have learned to accept it. I have learned one thing that's very important: if you don't make mistakes, you don't become a better person. I have made tons of mistakes. I could have done things better. I could have been richer if I had done things better. I could have had a bigger company if I had done things better and not made mistakes. But I did okay, based on what I had.

I had no real peer support at all. I was on my own, making my own decisions, and learning as I went. After my divorce, I was concentrating on the kids, and I worked out of my basement for years with my consulting business. When I started my own company — linking independent automated teller machines to the Interac electronic banking network — I ran the system twenty-four hours a day. I was not only the president and CEO, but also the main employee. It was a rags-to-riches story.

Through the first couple of years I was tied to our rent-subsidized townhouse. I was broke. I was out of a job and drained from my legal battle. Like a lot of my neighbours, I was on social assistance. Because I was a man I couldn't, at that time, get all of the assistance a woman could have got. It seemed very unfair, very wrong, but I didn't have the energy or willpower to fight it. Nobody would help me financially. I was on my own.

Finally, I started earning a trickle of income from consulting work. Every experience I have had has created determination in me, and that period was especially motivating — which is a positive way of saying it was very difficult. It made me more determined, more confident, and gave me more faith in who I was. It made me very focused as far as results and achievement are concerned.

Today I am financially very comfortable because of my kids, because I wanted to give them everything, and I was determined to work hard to get it.

When I was a kid and my mother was studying social work at McMaster, I remember seeing this movie about psychologist Harry Harlow's experiments with Rhesus monkeys and dolls. The experiments involved separating baby monkeys from their mothers and testing how they behaved with a wire mother shape, rigged up with a bottle of milk, compared to a soft, cloth mother that had no bottle. As it turned out, by far the monkeys preferred the mother who provided comfort to the one who provided food. The monkeys that had a cloth mother were not only happier, but also healthier. I saw that movie when I was maybe eight or nine, and it's stuck with me all my life. To me the lesson was that if you treat children better, they will do better.

Seeing that movie taught me that when it was my turn to have kids I had to give them the best possible environment, and I tried my best. It's like if you're born in a poor part of the city, the odds are you'll maintain that same lifestyle. I wanted to make sure I'd shown my kids that they could achieve a nice lifestyle and have a happy home. You know: monkey see, monkey do. I just wanted to give them a good environment, which I think I've done.

The kids went to a YMCA preschool program at first, and I met a lady there named Val, who eventually became a private nanny for the kids. With her in the picture, I had time to start doing more consulting work for financial institutions. I started selling some hardware from the States, including encryption devices for making bank cards. Money was dribbling in: a few thousand bucks in the first year, a few more the next year, a little more the year after that.

My real success would come way down the road in 1996, after I started TNS Smart Network, the company I just sold.

The children had an interesting life with me. Having Val as a nanny not only allowed me the chance to work, but it also gave me the opportunity to return to the dating scene. I dated several women over the years. I know I made some poor choices, along with a couple of very good ones.

I encouraged the kids to be very independent. I didn't spoil them a lot, but just enough. They certainly felt free to speak their minds. The funniest comment came from my daughter when she was a teenager and she asked, "When are you going to start dating women who are smarter than me?"

My entry into the consulting field had coincided with the boom in electronic banking, a field in which I was very comfortable. I knew the technology, I knew the system, and I was very comfortable selling. Basically, I would call financial institutions and ask, "Do you need any help?"

After spending so much time at the credit union, I had a lot of valuable knowledge about these things. I started bringing smaller banks into the Interac network. I had some contracts with banks and did a little better, bit by bit. I got really good experience in the banking sector and started to make a name for myself, and was thinking about creating a private service bureau for credit unions to run their ATMs and making some money from that.

I had been doing some work with a company in the United States that sold switches, or software that processed transactions between point A and B. If you went to an independent ATM, it would carry the transaction to your bank for processing. At that time there weren't any white-label ATMs in Canada yet, and they were just starting up in the United States.

Then I got a fateful call from the federal Competition Bureau, which was interested in tapping my expertise in running ATMs as they prepared to open the field to independent, third party operators, beyond the banks. They called and talked to me, and the opportunity suddenly arose. They asked about other people running ATMs. Would it be hard? Would it be a security threat? Could guys like me do this sort of shit? It seemed to me that they wanted reassurance that it would be okay.

I thought, "Holy shit! What an opportunity! I can do this."

They said they were opening up the market to more competition. I thought that was my chance, and decided to make a move.

The problem is that now my cancer marker is all the way back up to 318. Last month, it was at 190. In four weeks, it will be six hundred, then twelve hundred. It's doubling. The question is: what do you do next? The cancer is mutating. The particular regime I'm following isn't working anymore. Would it make any difference if I stopped it right now? I don't know. I could stop it and the numbers would continue rising at the same pace, or they could go faster, or they could slow down. I don't know. It's sort of like you're falling off a building and you don't know if anyone's going to catch you. Between the doctors and everyone I've hired, somebody has to come up with a solution. I'm even getting a second opinion on my Chinese doctor's opinion.

CHAPTER 6
Make It So

What was so funny about the whole white label industry was that it wasn't regulated, and it still isn't. It had no oversight. Interac was an association, so it had its own bylaws but there was no government body asking, "What are you doing with this money?" or "How are you doing this?" We ran the company very honestly, but if you didn't want to be honest you could have gotten away with murder. Here I was, as recently as this spring, moving $6 billion a year with no oversight. Bizarre, bizarre, bizarre.

I named the company TNS Smart Network, though I'm not really sure why. TNS doesn't mean anything, I just made it up. There's no fucking reason. It just sounded good, like something real. TNS, PMS, what the hell. I have no idea. There were other companies with longer names, but I didn't want one of those.

The start-up was a little rough. I had only $5,000. I went to all my friends and family and asked, "Would you give me some money to help start up my business?" All of them said no. So I went another way. I bartered. I bartered a percentage of the company for space in a building. I bartered shares for software and encryption devices. I owned forty-one percent of the company; the rest was divvied out in barter. I started with one part-time staff member and within twelve years worked up to forty-two staff, and the largest network of stand-alone, or white-label, machines in Canada, moving billions of dollars' worth of transactions through thirteen thousand machines every year, and making a piece of every transaction fee in the process.

The four shareholders, including me, started by putting some modems and software together to run a few ATMs. I was president and CEO, but I wasn't sure where I was going with it. All I knew was that if you build it they will come, and that's exactly what happened.

The model I wanted was that I was going to be the processor — the guy who runs the software that directs the transactions — and an ISO (independent sales organization) that gets the machines into their locations. The ISO goes out and sells the ATMs and makes most of the money. I wanted it to be combined. I tried to buy some machines for myself, but unfortunately, because the machines were so expensive and the industry wasn't yet there to quantify itself, I couldn't swing the financing.

What happened instead was that I entertained ISOs. People or companies would come to me and say, "I'd like to join TNS and I can put ten ATMs out there." I would sign you up as an independent sales organization, and you would hook up your ATMs to my computer system and I would process transactions. The ISOs worked as a third party sales force.

They would go to the ATM manufacturers and decide which company's machines they were going to associate themselves with. They'd buy ATMs — which used to go for $16,000, compared to $3,000 or $4,000 today — and put them in their stores.

The ISOs make their own arrangements with the people at the locations. There were a couple of models, and the amount of work you did would determine how much of the income you would keep. In one, retailers would buy the ATMs and put them in their stores. If they loaded their own money into the machines, they'd make the majority of the fees. There was the $1.50 or $2 service charge at the machine, and the interchange fee that the user's bank would charge. Interac would pay me my share of that fee, too. From the service charges and interchange fees, I would pay Moneris, the bank-owned gateway that hooked me up to Interac, and I would pay the ISO. If the ISO ended up with $1.50 from the surcharge and fifty cents from the interchange, they would decide out of that two dollars how much the merchant would get, depending on whether the ISO owned the machine or the merchant owned the machine, and other variables, like whose cash was in the machine, and who loaded it in. I wasn't involved in that, except in the early years, when my friend Frank and I had a side company that we operated as an ISO. We had about fifty-five of our own high-value machines in variety stores and gas stations. We ended up selling the company for a million bucks. We had a lot of fun and it was great to have an early success.

After that I was strictly a pimp for transactions. It was great. In the beginning, I was making good money: thirty to forty cents per transaction. That has shrunk to six or seven cents per transaction today. But there are differences. Back then I was doing a few thousand transactions a month. By the time I sold the company, I was close to five million transactions a month on thirteen thousand machines — thirty-five percent of Canada's white-label machines — moving $6 billion a year.

My best locations were casinos, because of the volume. Casinos are all about money, and ATMs are there to provide that money. ATMs can make more money per square foot than gambling machines can. The average white label ATM does about 270 transactions a day, while in a casino that's up into the thousands. It's a whole different world.

Setting aside all of the mechanics, the concept of TNS was very simple. A transaction would come in and get approved or declined by the bank. The approval message would come back to the merchant and the money would go out of the ATM. The only other step was that we'd have to make sure that the money from the financial institutions for the transactions would get back to the merchants the next day.

My business was that simple, at least in principle.

When I first started the company it had nothing but problems. It crashed, it burned, it died. We had software problems, and we had to create another division of the company, Smart Processing Solutions, to make our own software. Finally, we ended up building a piece of software that was secure, robust, and all those sales words that you use to say it worked very well.

The whole premise of my company was to be invisible. It had to work all the time. It needed to be reliable enough to become practically invisible.

Succeeding was a matter of hiring the right people to get things done. Some of the original employees I hired for TNS are still there today and they're good employees.

There wasn't any magic to TNS. There was a lot of politics, which I enjoyed getting involved in. There was a lot of dealing with ISOs, who always seemed to have bigger ideas of how many machines they were going to sell than they really could. Most of them were typical Canadians who wanted to get involved in setting up ATMs.

I ran my business trying to keep my clients, the ISOs, happy. I had learned that even if you have to mystify them, you have to keep them happy. Tell them what they need to know, keep yourself invisible, and they won't bother you. When they heard about something, I'd tell them not to worry about it, that I would take care of everything, and I did. You would sign up with me and do your thing. I would provide the service as reliably and efficiently as I possibly could. I tried to keep it a no drama company.

I made it seem like a magic trick, though there was no magic to this company at all, just discipline. I told my staff: make it work perfectly. There is no room for error. You can't be down for five minutes or you're dead.

It's just like with your cable or satellite TV. You can watch TV all year round and then once the screen goes blank and it says, "Searching for satellite," you say, "What crappy service." It's done its job for 365 days, but when it goes down for twenty minutes that doesn't matter any more. It's the same thing in the ATM world. If the ATMs go down at a casino for an hour, they don't care that it's been going perfectly four thousand hours straight. They only care that it's down now. You have to make sure that the customer is never affected by mistakes.

My biggest triumph was when they tried to bring the GST into my industry. They wanted to apply the GST to each transaction. I became very political. I did everything I could to fight the GST, and I won. That was about the time people came to call me the General out there.

I had a great time running that company, with a few exceptions. It was a very multicultural place, and I especially liked that.

Employees can be tough to work with though, and I was a tough boss, a real micromanager. If you were working with me, I would do things like go through the phone bills line by line, call people in and ask, "Why were you talking to this person for thirty-seven minutes?" When I saw that a guy in IT was making twenty-five phone calls a day to his mother, I called him on it. I had a guy working for me and his wife was pregnant. I went through his telephone bills, and there were these calls to 1-900 numbers from his company cell phone — adult, singles type of lines. You know what he said? "But I kept it under the one hundred minutes, so you didn't get charged anything extra."

He didn't get it. He thought it was about staying inside the one hundred minute plan we had. I said the point is you can't use your work phone for your self-gratification, especially when you have a pregnant wife at home. I thought, "What the fuck?"

To me, it's straightforward: if you're working for me from nine to five, then you should be working that whole time. After that, you can do what you want to do. If you want to put in more hours, that's great. You'll move up the ladder much more quickly. I had a very loyal staff. There was a lot of turnover through the years because I expected certain things from my management and if they didn't deliver, goodbye. By the end of my time there, there were three or four people from the original TNS still there. After twelve years, that's pretty good.

I don't mean to make it sound like it was a harsh climate. Everybody was on a, "Hi, Mischa" basis. I'd take the staff out every few months. We'd all go bowling or to Yuk Yuk's or a concert, something like that.

Another thing about my working style is that I don't believe in meetings. I'm one of those people who believe you should be able to resolve problems in ten minutes and move on to the next topic. When you come to a meeting, you should know the problem to be solved and have all the recommendations ready, discuss them quickly, and come to the point. It shouldn't take very long.

If your company has too many meetings, you're not working, you're not selling, and you're not growing. You're just spending your time in meetings.

You should have two meetings a week, forty-five minutes each. That's all you need. That's how I ran my company. You talk to people all the time and they're always saying, "I have to go to a meeting." What the fuck is there to talk about at so many meetings?

Having too many meetings is a symptom of having too many employees. I find that once you get over forty employees, the whole dynamic changes. People do less work. You get less out of each person.

⊙═╪═⊙

No company is all up, up, up. When I ran TNS, we had crises from time to time — nothing huge other than day-to-day crap that we had to resolve. My buddy Frank is a banker and thinks differently than me. I'm an entrepreneur. He's corporate. He sees four walls and runs a certain distance within those walls. When I ran my businesses, those walls moved huge distances all the time. You've just got to make decisions that bring those walls back into alignment. TNS had its moments, like any business. The system would crash, or something would happen and we would be down for a day, but that's business. It's not ideal, but it's normal. You deal with those problems and you get better.

We always had enough cash to keep going. I had one or two huge ISOs leave at one point, which pushed me to the edge of my cash flow, but we adjusted. They wanted to get a few more cents from a competitor, and that's what happens in business. By the time I sold the company, I had changed my strategy, so that instead of having a few big customers, we had 140 smaller customers, so that even if two or three decided to leave, it wouldn't hurt the bottom line. That reduced our exposure.

⊙═╪═⊙

When I first started TNS, I had a little office with three spaces, and over the years it grew to half the floor of the office building we were in Etobicoke, beside Highway 427. There were forty-three employees by the time I sold it. It was a typical office: the comptroller and my secretary and I sat in the executive area, the sales staff had another area, and the operations people had their area, plus an operations room where there were computers that showed all the transactions going down.

In the early years, I was there all the time, then gradually less and less as I was travelling more, visiting clients. By the end, I was going in only once or twice a week because I was working mostly from my phone and BlackBerry. I wasn't running the business by then. I was managing it, and I was doing it my way.

My main philosophy of management comes from the Jean-Luc Picard character in *Star Trek*. I don't believe presidents and CEOs should interact with their companies every day. Not at all. If you hire good management, they run your ship for you. That's what I did. I hired good people. At the end, I only went to work a couple of hours a week. I don't like to work. Who the hell wants to go to work? People who work nine, ten hours a day? Get a life. There's more to life than working. It's a piece of shit, working. Whoever came up with the concept is an idiot. You take a shit, have a shower, go to work all day for X number of dollars, and come home at the end of the day, then do the same routine over and over, what the hell kind of life is that?

In *Star Trek: The Next Generation*, Captain Picard would say to Number One, "I want to go to Planet X. Make it so." Then he would go to his ready room. What would he do in his ready room? He would read his books, learn about things. Not that I read a lot, but I don't want to be confined to the political bullshit of the running of a business traditionally. I like to run a business the way I like to run a business. I'm president and CEO, and my crew — my shipmates — are going to run the ship. Otherwise I'll hire somebody else. That's what I did.

I love being a shit disturber. I think it's the only way you get anywhere in this world. It's funny when I hear people complain without being prepared to do anything. If we are complacent, then we are the ones to blame for things being the way things are. I try to shit disturb for a positive reason, and I'm very good at it. I'm the type of person who sends emails from hell. I've done that a lot of times. I would send emails to my vendors that would say, "What the fuck did you think were you doing? I'm Mischa Weisz and I run this company. We're the biggest company and we do things this way and I expect this, this, and this, and don't you fuck it up." I would send it to the person and the person's boss and the boss's boss. I did it to create an environment where I could negotiate. When you get people riled up, they don't know how to deal with it very well, and that opens up the climate for getting what you want. That was my technique: stir the pot and get what I wanted. It worked every single time.

People don't know what to say when you do something unexpected, but it sure shakes things up and kind of resets the dial, which can create an advantage. Even when it doesn't, it's fun. I always try to bring people down to Earth, no matter who they are. Guess what? We're all the same. I don't care how much money somebody has.

Your shit stinks just as badly as mine stinks. In the end, we all die.

Building TNS was fun. I enjoyed doing that. I trail-blazed that whole industry. I'm the guy who brought the white-label network to Canada, who fought the government on the GST and won. I had no oversight. I had nobody watching me. I had to make up my whole world and decide what was best. For twelve years of my life, I had to invent rules to make sure that money got to the consumer and that the consumer's money got to the merchants.

The whole marketplace is changing now. There are new electronic chip cards coming in, new anti-money laundering rules that are tough, new forms of cards coming in. Visa, Interac, and MasterCard are at war. It's getting too complex. I built a lot of banks into the ATM world, but when I saw things getting too complex I knew I wouldn't be able to make the same kind of money in the same way three years from now, unless I had a lot more capital and changed everything. It was the perfect time for me to get out, and I had someone who was interested in buying.

I went to the company that was looking at me and said, "I want this much money, I want it in cash, and I want this type of holdback. I want this date of closing," and it all worked out.

◦═╪═◦

When I see women stuck at home because they're on welfare it angers me, because they could do so much more for themselves, and be so much happier. I had two children. Nobody helped me. At all. I went to everybody and asked,

"Would you give me a thousand bucks or two thousand
bucks?" And everybody said no, so I had to do everything
on my own.

⊶⊷

It's very important for people to do something with their
lives and make some kind of impression on society, or else
what's the point?

Can we do more? I don't know. But there's going to be a point where there's no more anybody can do. Pancreatic cancer is what it is. You can't hold it off.

It's not like I'm going to die in two weeks, but we do have to do something. What we're doing right now isn't working any more. That's where I'm at.

I'm a realist. I'm drinking my teas, taking my pills, doing my chemos, and I think it should be doing something for me, but right now it feels like it isn't doing anything. The cancer is still in there, growing aggressively. It's disappointing, but now it's a matter of finding another solution.

CHAPTER 7
Beaches, Starting Lines, and Jackpots

I had a terrible lifestyle. I ate out three or four times a week.

I ate a lot of red meat, especially steaks. I smoked cigarettes and cigars off and on in my younger days. I never smoked in front of my kids, but I would quit for a few years then go back. I drank martinis. I was way overweight. I'm five foot six and I weighed 220 pounds. I was a porker. I was a breeding ground for things to go wrong. Still, I was having a great life.

I was playing at the casino a lot, and I still do today. I love it. It's a beautiful place to lose yourself. I don't have to think there. When I'm not there I'm usually thinking about a thousand things. That's the way I am. My mind is always jumping around. I like the casino because I don't have to think. It's an emptiness, a void that I like.

I play the slots at Niagara Fallsview Casino. I had started small, and then I became a big player, a bigger player, and then a really big player, to the point where I got to know the management crew. I play so much now that the casino sends a limo to my house to pick me up and drive me home.

Sometimes I'll make or lose $20,000 in a night. When they hear that, some people look at me and say, "You're fucked up."

I look at them and ask, "Do you play the stock market? Then you're fucked up. At least at the casino I know I'll lose most of the time. In the stock market, you don't know what the hell is going to happen."

The truth is that I play the stock market with the money I got from selling my company, and I do pretty well there. The money I get in the stock market I use to play at the casino. I gamble it in one area and use the proceeds to gamble in another. It's all gambling. It's taking something and trying to make more of it. Whether I make money or lose money on the stock market or at the casino, it's all about trying to beat something. That's what it's always been for me: can I beat this?

My longest stint at the slots has been twenty-six hours. I went through $1.4 million in and out of those machines over that time. It was the best time of my life. I wasn't sick then. I had a crowd watching, and a business associate with me was telling the spectators that I was a prince.

I play so much I get my picture in the casino news-letter's gallery of jackpot winners every month. I'll walk

While I go there for enjoyment, it's also true that getting to know how the casino worked sort of helped getting my own ATMs in there, simply from becoming familiar with the operation. That familiarity, in turn, helped my company become worth much more, and at the end of the day helped me to sell it. If I hadn't had the casino ATMs in my business, I would never have gotten the money I did. Now I look at it this way: I lost money to make money.

I've always thought if I could write off all my losses — and there were a lot of losses — for the fact that I am actually doing business to procure further interest for my company, then I would have a great court case, but why waste my money? The government wouldn't hear of it.

The casino basically made me a rich man at the end of the day, not from my gambling, but from my business.

○━━○

I'm happy that I don't have to worry about money any more. If I need something I can get it. I like to gamble and not worry about how much I'm winning or losing.

Most of all, having enough money means I know my kids will be okay. It comes back to that Rhesus monkey experiment. I wanted my children to have the equivalent of the cloth monkey. That's important to me.

Beyond that, money really doesn't mean much to me. It's a service item. Deep down inside, I am a hippie. Give me some drugs and a beach, and I'd be a happy man.

Just take a look at the cars I've owned. I could be driving anything, but all I really want is something that's decent and reliable. My first car was an MG Midget. Big mistake. Cost me a lot of money when I didn't have any. My next car was a 1967 Oldsmobile Cutlass, then a Datsun 310, then three Accords and three Accuras. I like toys and I've got enough money to have a lot of them, but there's a point where you say a TV is a TV and a car is a car. Give me something that works and that's all I care about.

Would I like to have a Lamborghini? Sure, that would be fun. But in the end it would probably be uncomfortable, cost me a fortune in gas, and not even have room for my golf clubs. A car is a wonderful machine, but in my mind the first time you go to a parking lot and somebody opens a door into it, it's ruined. That's it. The car is worthless because of that one dent. It's just a car after that. If I did that with a $200,000 car, I'd be neurotic.

<hr/>

I like women and people know me for that. I'm like Alfie, or at least I was. You remember that movie? I could relate to Michael Caine's character. I've had many, many, many girlfriends, and my kids have criticized me for that. What's interesting and comforting is that both my kids have good relationships of their own right now. Better than I ever did. I find that intriguing.

Women and I are two very different creatures. I've come to understand that. One thing I've learned is that they need the "S" words — safety and security — which men don't need, at least not to the same degree. We do in a certain way, but not to the extent women do. No matter what kind of women they are, or how powerful or intelligent, they need that. I probably do a shitty job of providing it. I'm intelligent, so that's good for a while, but because of my weirdness, as some have called it, the security probably isn't too good.

I like women. I enjoy the company of women. I enjoy getting dressed up and doing stuff with them. I like good-looking women. Period.

I like women, physically. Mentally, I have a harder time relating to them. From my perspective, it's because women always like to have drama. Life has enough drama without looking for it. I like normal: here's my space, here's my toilet paper. You know? Unnecessary drama is not something I'm good with. Jerry Springer, CNN, anything that's overly dramatic, I'm out. I like normal. That's probably why I've had a lot of women.

I also like guy time, though not just with anyone. I prefer to have a few people I'm very comfortable with in my life, rather than a lot of people who I don't know and trust as well. I listen to people talk about stuff, but I quickly run out of capacity to deal with bullshit. It annoys the living shit out of me when people talk and don't know their facts, but force their opinions on you anyway.

At least with men, I can say whatever I want and get away with it, and they don't get prissy. With women, you've got to be more careful. I used to say and do things in the office that you wouldn't believe. I'm surprised human rights people didn't come in and shut me down a dozen times. Our office, it was like *Ally McBeal*. Everything got pushed to the line.

With men, I can get away with a lot of shit. With women, I have to be more careful, but I still get away with a lot.

I have always tried to do nice things with my kids, even when I had to stretch to make things happen. At first it was hard to find the money. Later, it was hard to find the time, but we always found a way to do it. We went to Disney many times. We went to Italy.

Through it all, we went camping at Port Elgin, on Lake Huron, sometimes with our friends, like Frank and Linda Helt, or Paul and Jackie Buckle, and sometimes on our own.

We spent so much time at Port Elgin that I finally bought a cottage there ten years ago. But before that, in the first years after I got separated, I took the kids camping there. There's nothing worse than having toddlers going into the water and bringing back half the lake in their diapers, but I enjoyed it.

One of the neatest things that ever happened there was that one night on a camping trip we were lying on the beach, staring up at the stars, and the sky started to flutter. What it became over the next few hours was the northern lights. It was a neat experience for the kids and me, and I'll always remember it as a magical night.

Camping was great, but one day I thought, I'm too old for this shit. I called a real estate agent in Port Elgin and I said, "I'm coming up there. I want to look at eight places and I want to buy something." And that's what I did. I wanted a cottage for the kids, and I bought one in 1999. We'd go up several times a year. It meant that there was always a place where the kids could to go have some fun on the beach.

Lately though, we hadn't been going as much. My daughter is in Victoria, and my son is here, but he's busy and I'm sick, so I sold it. It's one of those things. I would love to have kept it, but it just wasn't practical. When you have cancer, you start to bring closure to things. I sold the cottage to Frank's brother, Robert. I used to rent it to his family for a couple of weeks every summer, and they got to like it there. I like knowing they're there now.

Another reason I sold the cottage was that I've got a wonderful landscaped yard here at home, with a swimming pool and a hot tub. Driving up there and setting everything up became a burden for me. It was a pain in the ass, unless the kids were going to be there.

The kids already say they miss it, which is kind of cool in a way, because it proves that those times were important to them.

For us, going to Port Elgin was always a time when we got to be together, to be on the beach. The dog was there. It was like that ideal family thing to do. I tried to make that dream come true, for me as much as for my children. It might be a strange way to see it, but I was trying to correct what I thought I had missed out on when I was a kid. I tried to compensate, and I think I succeeded. They have memories. I know it, because when I'm driving them and I hear the two of them in the back seat talking, they're saying things like, "Remember when we did this? Remember when you got in trouble for that?" It brings a smile to my face, because they're remembering. They have much better memories than I do.

When the kids were younger, they used to make me cards that showed stick figures of three people and a dog. That was us, and it made me happy to see how they were thinking of us as a family. There's a sculpture I have in my living room today that shows a parent and two children holding hands. My son gave that to me three years ago, as a teenager. I know my kids think a lot about how we work as a family. That means a lot to me.

Was I lovey-dovey as a father? At times, but not a lot. Was I cold and distant? No. Was I practical as a parent? Yeah. I probably was. We did things together. We held hands together. I would hold them when they cried. I wasn't an overly loving parent, but I'm not generally that way with anyone. I think I've been a good parent. It's strange to reflect on these things. I was hard on my kids. I would punish them if they weren't good. I wouldn't tolerate them talking back or that kind of shit. But in terms of discipline, I was far more relaxed than my father and mother. I allowed my kids to have their friends over, and do all the things that I think kids should have a chance to do. One thing that shows me they had a successful childhood is that they learned how to network.

Networking, to me, is success in life. Kids who don't grow up knowing how to network don't do well. They live in their own little worlds and when they grow up they stay that way. Networking is being able to interact with other people. I was shy when I was a kid and I didn't interact very well with people at all. Only later, when I was in high school and moving out, did I have to learn these skills. That was when I realized networking is a survival skill. It gets you friends. It gets you jobs. Networking is what life is all about. Society doesn't grow if people don't network. It helped me in my career.

When I decided to give some of my money to charity early in 2009, it was easy for me to give it to the YMCA,

Top: *A family portrait of Mischa, Nathan, and Danielle.* Bottom: *Close family friend Dina.*

Top: *Nathan, Danielle, and Mischa.* Bottom: *Danielle with Sierra, the family dog.*

Top: *Mischa hanging out in the kitchen.* Bottom: *Danielle shows off her red highlights.*

Top: *Nathan and Mischa pose in a parking lot.* Bottom: *Nathan at the lake.*

Top: *Connie and Mischa's wedding kiss.* Bottom: *Connie and Mischa's wedding toast.*

Top left: *Frank Helt and his wife, Linda.* Top Right: *Mischa and Frank Helt.* Bottom: *Connie and Mischa, happy together.*

Top: *Mischa, Danielle, and Nathan.* Bottom left: *Paul Buckle and his wife, Jackie.*
Bottom right: *Mischa and Paul Buckle.*

Top: *Mischa and Guido as they are today.* Bottom: *A studious Mischa and Guido.*

especially for children's community outreach programs. The Y helped me as a kid and later helped me with my kids. The YMCA here in Hamilton has created a Mischa Weisz Endowment Fund with the $500,000 donation I made. That way, I know that over the coming years and decades, a lot of kids will get a better shot at succeeding, and I feel good knowing I'll have a hand in that.

I'm a great believer in free enterprise, but I believe in one thing that's really liberal: everybody has the right to start at the same starting line. Where you go from there is up to you.

That's why I gave to the Y, and that's where my parents' NDP influence comes in. I think every society has an obligation to ensure that all people have the ability to make something of themselves. The only way you can do that is to empower them to be at a level where they can start: to get an education or to start a business. That's the socialist side of me. It's like a race, though. If they fail, it's their problem. Still, everyone should have that same beginning. Not everybody gets the chance to choose, and it's important to me that everybody should have a chance at a good start. If we could guarantee that, we'd have a serious chance at getting rid of poverty, starvation, and slums. It's important that we as a society do something like that.

The funny thing about socialists and conservatives is that socialists don't think anybody should be rich. But in the capitalist world, there are people who are rich, and they fund a lot of things that are important to everyone. If you didn't have those people, you wouldn't have these things, or at least not to the same extent. If you didn't have those people you wouldn't have things like the Juravinski

Cancer Centre, serving an area of nearly two million people in Hamilton and the rest of southern Ontario. The centre started with a big donation from two business people, Charles and Margaret Juravinski. At the end of the day, you have to give a reasonable helping hand to people.

At the time I decided to donate to the YMCA, I was being hit up for donations by a lot of people at different charitable foundations. In every case, I asked myself: who am I really helping? I didn't have the same confidence in the others as I did in the YMCA.

If I make donations for children, those children will all have a chance to get to the starting line. That feels pretty good.

I feel like shit the day after a chemo treatment. It's been changing. At first, it was no problem. I even got up and went to Vegas two hours after the first one. As time has gone on, the chemo and my body have been reacting differently. In the last month or two, I have been having slight fevers after my treatments, which I'd never had before. It was getting to the point where I couldn't go to the casino after a treatment — and that was a crisis of Biblical proportions for me. I'd take a Tylenol 3 or a Demerol, and feel one hundred percent better. I've tried to stay away from pain pills, but those are so benign, it's okay. If I feel like shit, I just take one.

There are a few other side effects of the chemo. If I look at the skin on my arm, for instance, I don't feel heat or cold evenly anymore. Some areas will be much more sensitive, others barely sensitive at all. It's called neuropathy. It's very discomforting.

CHAPTER 8
Empty Nest

My own kids are both like me. It's a split. If I was made of sand and you dumped me out, the sand would pour in two different directions into my kids. They have similar qualities and different ones, but I see myself in both of them. Each kid is stronger in some areas. My daughter Danielle is very artistic. She has been trained as a makeup artist to make monsters and other creatures for the movies. She did it for nine months and got her certificate for that. I think it's very, very cool. Today she lives in Victoria and seems very happy there. Nathan and I just went out to visit her.

My daughter's not a born salesperson. She's more of a hands-on type, with a deep inner sense, a very powerful personality, and a strong will. She will send me an email saying, "Dad, I think you promised me a PS3. Where is it?" She'll even tell me to fuck off, which I think is cool. She and her brother Nathan are both very intelligent. They're survivors.

My daughter is the princess of her own little world, though she would fight me on that. She is confident, but also not confident. She certainly has a bold exterior. She went Gothic as a teenager, or at least semi-Gothic. Always wearing black, and deliberately trying to be shocking. I recognized the behaviour, because I used to be that way.

One day, a couple of years ago, she came over here around Halloween and made cookies that were supposed to look really gruesome. She did it for shock value and for fun. I knew there was nothing wrong with my daughter. She's got her act together, and she always has, but she wanted to shock me. She has always loved to talk, talk, talk, and talk. I remember her as a really outgoing kid. Nathan, on the other hand, was very shy.

Neither of my kids seemed motivated to crawl as babies. They sat there. They did not want to move. It was like they sat there until they were nearly two years old and then decided to walk. I wondered if they were just lazy, like me. They like to work, but if they didn't have to they wouldn't.

I think Nathan is going to be more of the entrepreneur, networking his way around. He'll be the salesperson. He's a buddy-buddy type of guy, with a kind of a crazy streak. He's the social one and likes to have people around all the time. He's the opposite of me in that way. I don't need to have people around all the time.

As a kid, he was noisy and needed attention, like his sister, and I was happy to give it to him. I took Danielle to dance and piano class. I took Nathan to piano, too, but he never wanted to do his homework, even though I tried to help him. I took him to soccer, and I got so mad at him. He was out there talking to the members of the other team while they were supposed to be playing. He was socializing! I said, "What are you doing? You're not friends with these guys at this point. You're supposed to be trying to beat them!" That's the way he was. He was always more interested in socializing. He is a very carefree spirit, but both of them have a real intensity to them.

Nathan lives near downtown Hamilton, near the first place I lived in after I moved out. He's in a condo, which I'm paying for. He couldn't live here anymore. You know why? He's a slob. The man is a slob. It drove me nuts. He also developed the idea that he should be able to come and go whenever he pleased, and I said, "You know what? If you're not going to follow the rules, you need to be on your own, so you can figure out how life really works."

His condo is beautiful. It has a white carpet — which probably isn't white any more. I want him to appreciate the fact that being on your own isn't the greatest thing in the world. You have to do everything for yourself.

These days, Nathan and I are spending a little more time together, and we enjoy ourselves. We get each other, too, and you have no idea how satisfying that is. I recently took him to see the new Star Trek movie. It was a small moment, but an important one. I know he's busy, and I'm busy, but at the end of the day, he knows there are certain things you have to do.

I don't hear from my son or my daughter as much as I would like to, but I know they think about me a lot.

I'm okay with that, because when they do call we talk normally. You can end up dying without talking to your son or your daughter, which is a terrible thing to have happen. Terrible. But we are talking and we do have a reasonable relationship.

When I look back on my life with my kids, it's a blur. It just happened. I'm very happy, though. I think about the trips. I think about Port Elgin.

I used to wonder: do you need to have two parents to have a family? No, you don't. I found that out. When they would write me cards, they would draw little pictures of themselves and of me. I'm happy with the course I took with my kids. I really am.

I often try to guess — I'm not going to be able to see it, unfortunately — what kind of people my kids will be like ten years from now? Will they be like me? Will they be like their mom? Will they be something else altogether?

My daughter is now in a routine where she calls me every week, which is very cool. We talk. The nice thing is we can say whatever we want. We're getting each other, and that's great. When we're on the phone and we're about to hang up I do something that really bugs her. I say, "I love you." She has a hard time saying it back, but she does it. It's pretty tough for a twenty-one-year-old, but I force her into it, and I think it's good for both of us.

I have no regrets as a parent. I have regrets with women, but I have no regrets with my kids. At the end of the day, I listen to them, and I know they're good shits. They're okay. They're going to be fine.

Do I wish they were living here at home with me while I am sick? That's complicated, but the short answer is that I think they should be doing what they want to do. I miss them. I wish I had that *Leave It to Beaver* family, but they did the same thing I did. I hope they'll have a better concept of family values than I did. I love both my children and I know both my children love me.

We had a lot of fun.

I've been looking at a lot of our videos lately, and with a little distance I can see they had a normal childhood. There was nothing exceptional, and I'm proud of that. I'd thought many times, "There's no mother here. How's that going to play?" But our nanny Val's presence helped to make up for a lot of that.

Another very positive influence on their childhood was the presence of a woman I was dating during some of their most important years of growing up, Dina. We were together for four years, from 1997 to 2001, starting when Danielle and Nathan would have been nine and seven. She was bubbly, bright, and cheerful. She really liked to have fun. She was there at Christmas when the kids were opening their presents, and she travelled with us on vacation. Dina was a lovely person, and I was very much in love with her. Not that we didn't have our ups and downs like any other relationship.

The thing with Dina and me was that we had two relationships. One was on the personal side and one was on the business side, and I think they fed off each other. Dina worked for the Bank of Montreal in an area called gateway services, which provided access to Interac for other financial institutions. I'd pay a fee to the Bank of Montreal to get that access for my own clients at TNS. Dina helped me get through some of the doors I had to get through to help my business work, and she took pride in the fact that she helped me to grow that business.

I remember the first date we had. She said, "Why don't we meet at Jonathan's Restaurant in Oakville?" It was her suggestion.

One thing I hate is people being late. It's a pet peeve with me, especially with my employees who were tardy. I'd say, "You want to start at ten after nine? Great. I'll start paying you at ten after nine."

Anyway, she was late for our first date. While I was waiting, I started drinking martinis. By the time she showed up I was on my third martini, with no food. But we still had fun.

During our time together, I know she had a hard time understanding who I was. She wanted me to be more straightforward. I don't like things to be simple. I like adventure. I'm the kind of guy who likes to get into the sailboat first and then decide where to go.

The other challenge for her was that that she was going out with me, but also working in the department that served my competitors, and that was interfering. Her job was really important to her and she felt it brought her close to a conflict. Eventually, she moved into a different area.

My adventures in travelling really started because of Dina. She exposed me to going on island vacations and cruises, and things that I had never done before.

She also introduced me to the casino. Back then, the Bank of Montreal had some machines in the casinos, and Dina had the contract at Fallsview. She got me hooked. I would play with maybe $100 at the smaller casinos. By the time I started going to Fallsview, I was playing big.

Later, when Dina's contract ended, I won the new contract at Fallsview and put my own machines in there, acting as an ISO. Putting those machines into the casino made my company a lot more valuable. Landing the Fallsview account gave it real punch, and I can say it was indirectly because of Dina.

After we broke up, we stayed in touch as friends. We would call each other once a week and talk about life and business. She met another man, named Larry, and they got along well, and it was nice to see.

But in 2005, Dina got sick. It was pancreatic cancer. We saw each other regularly until the last couple of months. She married Larry in the summer of 2006. She died in September of that year, almost a year to the day before I was diagnosed with the very same thing.

A few months after Dina died, I lost another friend, Clayton Long, to pancreatic cancer. Clayton, Frank Helt, and I had been partners on a project where we had bought some land in Southampton to develop. Clayton only lasted a few weeks.

When I found out about my own pancreatic cancer, I'd already had two people relatively close to me die from the same thing. Statistically, thirty-three thousand people in North America get pancreatic cancer each year, and I knew two of them within a year, and then myself. Pretty weird.

The first thing I thought was, "I'm fucked. I'm done."

The surgeon had said I'd be dead within four or five months, and there was nothing they could do for me. I accepted that at first, because of the experience I'd had with those two other people in my life.

But I would soon change my outlook.

What baffles the doctors is that I still look healthy. I still have a gleam in my eye, even after fifty-seven chemos. Yes, I'm tired. That's where I am. It's an interesting adventure. I'm on this diet and I'm faced with this new challenge: the cancer is spreading in my lungs and in my liver. And I'm wondering, what do I do next? Do I go on stronger chemo? You have to be careful. There's a fine line where you have to keep your immune system strong and keep your mind strong enough to survive the chemo. When you cross that line to where the chemo is too strong and you hurt your immune system and you hurt your mind, you're fucked. You're done. And I've been so careful not to cross that line.

CHAPTER 9
Storm and Shelter

Connie and I met through an online dating service called eHarmony. She lived in Paris, Ontario, about thirty minutes west of Hamilton. Her children were grown and she was on her own. She was working as a comptroller, which showed me that she was intelligent. I could see from her picture that she was good looking. We went back and forth a little online before we finally started talking on the phone and going out in the spring of 2007. Once we started, we became close very quickly. I have a habit of doing that. Things were going really well, and we seemed to understand one another.

Within the first few weeks, I suggested we go on a vacation together to Jamaica. She was surprised, but she agreed.

Everything was great, and I fell in love with Connie. She is a strong, independent person and I like that. I tried hard to spoil her, which is a sign that I am really feeling happy around someone.

Connie and I have a very strong connection. More than once she has sensed I'd be calling at the very moment that I was dialing her number. We had even started to talk about getting married before I found out I was sick.

I'd been having a lot of doctor's appointments, trying to figure out what was wrong with me. She came with me to all my appointments. She was with me when I found out I had cancer and later, when I learned I could expect to live only four or five months. She cried quite a bit.

After such a short time together, a lot of people wouldn't stick around through something like that, but she did. There was never any question for her. It was exceptional that she would have such a kind heart to stay with me, and she is still with me to this day. Instead of abandoning our talk of marriage, we accelerated it.

In my own strange way, I thought I only had a few months to live and one of the things I'd wanted to do before I died was get married again. It was a very good relationship already, so I went to Connie and asked, "Would you marry me, even under these circumstances?" She said yes, so that's what we did.

We wanted to get married quickly and we went to a jewellery store to get a ring. When we found one we liked, the clerk said it would take a month to process the order. I told him that was too long, and I lied, telling him we needed it right away since she was pregnant — which Connie thought was hilarious. It was a serious time, but you always have to keep your sense of humour.

I was thrilled to be getting married. I knew I would be ending my life in a very nice situation: happy with a nice wife, and my kids entering their adulthood in a positive way.

We put the wedding together in a matter of a couple of weeks. We got married at the Olde School, a very nice restaurant with its own wedding chapel, just outside of Paris, Ontario. We had about thirty close family and friends there. It was a very nice little wedding, a civil ceremony. It was very romantic and it went very well.

Our relationship is more complicated than most because of our circumstances, but we work on it, and we're doing well. She comes to all my medical appointments with me, and takes care of most of the details of my treatments. Today, our relationship gives me a lot of solace. I know that somebody I love is going to be there holding my hand the whole time, and that means so much to me.

⚬━◆━⚬

So right around the time my relationship with Connie was starting to get serious, I had all this stuff going on with my body. I had developed diabetes, and I asked my doctor "what's wrong with me?" My blood sugar was going up and down and right and left. Now we know that was the beginning of the cancer, though it could have been anything. Who knows? If I had had a CAT scan a year before, maybe I could have been saved.

Once I got the prognosis from the surgeon that was it. I walked out without any drama. I'm not afraid to die. I'm not in a rush to go there, but I know that I've had a great life and I'm not upset about it.

There are four stages in cancer. My cancer was caught at Stage IV, the last stage. I had a four-inch tumour on my pancreas, and the cancer was all through my omentum, part of the membrane that encases all of your guts. It was in a couple of lymph nodes, and at first it was sort of, "Okay. I'm going to die." I went for chemo and had some positive responses, which was unusual.

Then I went farther. I wanted to explore all the possibilities, inside the hospital and out. My friend Frank and I have another friend called James Chan. He introduced us to a traditional Chinese doctor who practices herbal medicine in Markham. He doesn't know any English, so James came along as interpreter, and he's done that faithfully ever since.

The Chinese doctor put me on a regimen of the most disgusting shit I can possibly drink. You put all these stems and plants into this enormous teapot. It looks like a bird's nest in there and it brews for an hour. Every time I make it, I have to work up the nerve to drink it. It's like drinking water that's been run through a blend of road tar, compost, and an old man's pillow. Then I decided to go to the Block Center for Integrative Cancer Treatment outside of Chicago, where they put me on a strict diet and a regimen of pills, about one hundred pills a day. They took my blood, and measured the vitamins, and inflammatory agents in my body, stuff I don't really understand, and they gave me stuff to help counteract the various deficiencies in my blood system. The whole idea of working with cancer — I don't call it fighting cancer, I call it working with cancer — is that your immune system gets weak in certain areas, and you die.

So I was doing three things: the chemo, the herbs, and the pills. It's all complementary. As far as I know, all of it could be working, some of it could be working, or none of it could be working, but I have the means to try all of it, so that's what I'm doing.

I've learned a lot about cancer. Cancer is not like french fries at McDonald's. It's different for every single person, as far as how fast it's going to go, how it's going to respond to different medicines. That's why they haven't been that successful at curing cancer. There are too many different possibilities.

Naturally, I've spent a lot of time thinking about my cancer. I try to feel my body. I know that sounds really strange, but if your knee hurts, you know your knee hurts. I try to go into my organs. Call it meditation or whatever you want. I say to myself, "Okay. I feel like shit. What does that mean? Is it the cancer or is it something else?" I try to analyze where my body is. I do it all the time — lying in bed or anywhere.

I got in touch with a company that's going to do more specific processing of the molecular structure of my cancer, for $23,000. We don't usually do that in our healthcare system. We say, "You have cancer," and treat everybody the same and give them all the same drugs, hoping that some will survive and knowing that some won't. Can we do better than that? There's another theory out there that says cancer can't live in an alkaline state. If you think about it, red meat creates acidity. Sugar, fruit, cheese, they create acidity. Is there merit to it? I don't know, but I try it anyway. I look at the Internet every day to see what's new out there.

Every day I see people on the street and they say I don't look sick. I look healthier than I probably ever have.

Under the diet I have from the Block Center, all red meats disappear. All chicken and turkey disappears. Vegetables are okay. Fish is okay. No sugar. No milk. No cheese. No dairy products at all. Nothing white. Everything is brown: rice and noodles. I'm pretty good, though I cheat a little. If I go to a dinner and they have veal chops, I say, "Okay, what the hell." Do I think it will affect me at the end of the day? I don't know. The counts are going up, but I don't know why, so I don't know.

The thing I miss most is pepperoni sticks. They are the worst goddamned things for you, but I miss them. As the child of European parents, I was brought up eating foods that would make some people gag. But I like food. I enjoy it very much. I love pepper, which I don't eat any more, either, because my Chinese doctor said I am a hot person and should avoid spices and pepper at all costs.

I really miss meat. I wish I could have a steak, or prime rib, or chicken. I look at a menu now and after I rule out all the items I can no longer eat, it seems the same three things are always left: salmon, sea bass, and grouper. I've eaten so much salmon I can't even look at it any more. After two years of it, I've just had to stop eating it.

I don't admit to doing stupid things too often, but I made a big mistake with my eating. I've been making special shakes with exotic fruit juices — goji and noni juice. I break up my morning pills into them. For protein, I'd been adding whey powder. Then my friend Frank told me whey is made from milk! I went home and checked and realized I'd been having the equivalent of ten glasses of fucking milk when I wasn't supposed to be having any! I had misread the label or picked up the wrong can or whatever and thought I'd been taking soy the whole time. I'd been using it for months. Who knows what that did to me?

On the upside, I've increased my vitamin D to five thousand units a day, so I hope that's helping.

I don't feel that bad for someone who is supposed to be very ill. You know how when you work out and then at the end of the day you feel sore? That's how I feel now, but it's not that bad. I'm alert. I'm awake. I need massage, but otherwise I feel okay. I keep surprising myself and sometimes ask how I managed to get to this point.

I do feel myself getting more tired. This is not a sign that I'm giving up, because I am not, but I can see how some people get to the point where they say, "That's enough feeling like this."

I'm not afraid of dying, but I like the idea that I'm keeping it at bay. I don't know if it gets worse, if I'll have the diligence to maintain my mindset. At what point do you break as a human being? I've thought about that a lot. I wonder if I'll crack.

My body has been through a lot in the last two years. I started on one type of chemo, then I went on stronger chemo, then even stronger chemo, and I'm on pretty strong stuff now. The counts of my cancer marker are going up dramatically and that doesn't make me happy. It doesn't worry me as much as it frustrates me: what do I do next? I've done pills. I'm doing Chinese medicine. I've changed my diet. So what else can I do? I've just joined a pilot exercise program for cancer patients at the YMCA, called CanWell. I'm trying that, but I'm worried about exercise, because if you're lifting weights you're ripping muscles, and that creates weakness, and that's where the cancer wants to go.

I've found myself shorter of breath these days. I don't know if that's because the cancer is now in my lungs, or because it's psychological. That's one thing you have to fight: the mental battle. I take my cancer and set it aside as a third party. But I'm a human being and I do worry: will I break? I haven't cried about it, I haven't been sad about it. I have taken it very logically, as if it's a business situation: something is fucked up and I'm trying to fix it.

If I say the word cancer to you, what's your next thought? Death. You think you're going to die. That's the whole problem with cancer. People automatically associate it with that word: death.

One thing about people with cancer these days is that they're not dying as fast. They can be filled with cancer, but they're still living. Why is that? People are looking at alternatives, taking advantage of new medical developments, and taking better care of themselves. All of that helps their bodies stay stronger over longer periods, and that creates hope. I believe that hope plays a powerful role in extending people's lives.

I ask myself, could I handle anything better than cancer? Could I handle Lou Gehrig's disease? I don't know. I think I'd rather have cancer. Could I sit there in a wheelchair not able to move for five or ten years? I don't know. This way my quality of life, at least until the last three or four weeks, is going to be great, and then I'll die. Do I want to die at fifty-three? No. But then that's just the way things are. I look at things like this: I've had cancer for about two years. I've sold my business, and now I'm writing a book and doing a film about my life. None of this ever would have happened if I didn't have cancer. Everything happens for a reason. It all fits in perfect little pieces. So I'm never unhappy about the way it's happening.

I still have a busy life. I go out for dinner, to shows, and to the casino. I play golf. I have been to the Bahamas. I went to see the Super Bowl in Tampa Bay. I've been fly-fishing on the Bighorn River Montana and gone to see my daughter in Victoria. I stay up late watching TV.

Of course, in the middle of everything else, I have been passing kidney stones. I keep them when I can find them. They're bigger than I thought. The only good thing about having them is morphine. It makes everything feel better.

If I am not careful though, with everything I have going on I can get tired, and I do know I have to be careful.

My breathing is not great. My lung collapsed while I was getting it drained, and that was rough. The liquid keeps coming back. I don't like these things. In my mind, everything seems normal, but my body just isn't there.

One thing that really bugs me when I go to the cancer clinic is seeing people who go and get their chemo and then go out for a fucking cigarette. What part are you fucking not getting about cancer? You are idiots. As far as I'm concerned, the health system should refuse these people. They shouldn't get the treatment. They're wasting taxpayers' money. What's the point of trying to help them? A person has got to take some responsibility.

I watch how my friends handle what's happening to me, and there's such a range of reactions. Some people have a hard time asking directly: how are you doing? Some want me to live longer, but others are worried that I'll suffer for too long. It's nice to see people having emotions about it.

At the time I was diagnosed, I had been on the outs with my friends Paul and Jackie for years. We had argued at the cottage over some perceived slight. There was yelling and screaming, and they packed up and left. That was it. We didn't talk again for eight years, until I was diagnosed. It was silly. A stupid thing.

They called as soon as they heard about me being sick, and we immediately forgot about our quarrel. Closure is important to me, and I think it's important to them, too. I think it's important to everybody. We resumed our relationship like no time had passed. Years had gone by, but we were back and it was cool. We've known each other for more than forty years, and I just look on it as a little break. It's great to have everyone back together again. I just like sitting around with them, and Frank and Linda. That's what I like: just sitting around with my friends.

I can tell they're concerned about me. I know that they want to be there for me and I feel bad for them in a strange way, because they'll have to suffer through something when I die. I try to imagine how I would feel if one of those people disappeared on me. I don't even know how to contemplate it. It would be very bizarre. I get a lot of strength from my friends.

I also try my best to help myself by using my mind. When I go to bed at night, I turn on some meditation music, and I try to focus my concentration so I can look down into my body, into its energy, and I try to visualize my cancer.

The images I see with my mind's eye are very abstract. It's nebulous, it's chaotic, it's random. I try to find patterns and structure, and put some order to it by finding and destroying the cancer with the power of my consciousness. Imagine you're going down a tunnel and you hit something and try to break it apart. It's like that. I'll start by trying to direct energy through my body to my cancer. I'll try to visualize my own cells. I know it sounds hokey, but the mind is an amazing, tricky thing. It can drive us nuts, or it can bring us a tremendous amount of happiness. I think our state of mind controls our health in more ways than we realize. If you're an environment like a stockbroker's and you're losing money, you can get sick, or have a heart attack or jump out the window. I believe that to a certain extent you can help your body by using a positive mental approach to instruct the elements in your body to fight your cancer.

Another technique I use is to bring energy through my entire body, right town to my toes, so I can sit there and feel it. I do all this just before I fall asleep, so my mind can work on it all night. I used to think about sex. Now I think about cancer. See how far I've come? At first, when I did this I was very successful and it was really cool. But as time has gone on, I haven't been able to get to the colours and the place where the cancer is. I stopped for a while, wondering if maybe I'd done it too much.

I think a lot about fate. I do believe that there is a pre-ordained script for us, but it's often puzzling to wonder why it takes the directions it does. If we talk about the Holocaust, we ask, was it preordained? Why did it happen? Was it fate? Interesting questions.

Let's talk about God for a second. I'm not anti-religious, but from my perspective religions have caused more wars and more people to suffer than they have saved. I'm not just talking about the Second World War. I'm talking about much farther back in history. Religion was a way to justify so many things, even slavery. Religion has been a way to manipulate the masses and to restrict freedom of expression.

Religion is not important, in my opinion. I see it as a form of bias, and I don't like bias. People will go to church and be filled with "love thy neighbour" and then leave without having learned anything. That's why I don't believe in religion, though I do believe in fate. I ask myself, why is this cancer happening to me? Why don't I just die like most people die? I see it like this: I have an opportunity to enjoy my life, to tell my story and show that life isn't over because you have pancreatic cancer.

I can never say with absolute certainty that anything I've done has made a difference. Maybe even being positive hasn't made a difference. Maybe I have lived this long because of something else, like the particular form of my pancreatic cancer.

I would hope, though, that the things I've gone through — taking thousands of pills, drinking tea that tastes like it came out of somebody's asshole — have made a difference. I'd be kind of disappointed if there does turn out to be a God, and He says, "All those pills? That tea? That was all a joke!" That's the kind of thing that would happen to me.

If one thing has helped me to survive this long, I think it has been positive thinking. Everything I have done has been some kind of struggle. Living at home with parents I could never get completely close to, living through a difficult marriage and divorce, raising two children on my own, building businesses from almost nothing; all of it has been a struggle. But I have always had hope. Without that, the struggle will destroy you. I was determined that never, ever was a struggle going to destroy me.

I'm determined — not to live forever, but to see how long I can outlive this cancer. I find it an interesting game. It's no different than a slot machine. You put money in and you have no idea what it's going to put out. With cancer, you keep putting shit into your body, and you don't know if you're going to get a good reading or a bad reading. Right now, we're in a bad zone. Things are bad. That's interesting. Why did they go bad? What did I change? Should I go backwards? Am I not thinking about it properly? There are a thousand things going though my head. Maybe I've gotten careless and cheated on my diet too many times, instead of sticking to the original plan. It's time to assume that the chemo regime we've been using isn't working at its best any more. We've decided to go with something a little more effective. I'm on a chemo right now that out of ten is a two or a three, and I'll be going to one that is about a six.

CHAPTER 10
Building a Legacy

⊙━━━⊙

I sometimes sit and think about how I'm actually going to die.

I've always thought I'd go out by shit disturbing one last time, so I'm thinking of these as my last words, just before I close my eyes the final time: "Oh my God! I see the light! It's not what we think it is!"

That would really fuck everybody up.

Sure it's immature. But it's fun, and that is an important part of me. How do you make up Mischa Weisz? You take Alfie, Fred Flintstone, Archie Bunker, and the guy from *Family Guy* and at the end of the day you've basically got me.

Seriously though, I am thinking about my legacy. I can do it because I have the luxury of advance warning that a lot of other people never get, and that lets me plan. Planning gives me a feeling of control, and that is comforting in itself.

I'm the type of person who makes sure that on the day I disappear, everything will be nicely tidied up. It's just the way I am. Even my dog, Sierra, died on me a few months ago. She looked at me and I looked at her, and I said, "You're going first, I guess, eh? Okay."

I am doing this documentary, and I am planning to do a four minute video at my own funeral. I am doing this book, like the movie, because I want to take a positive approach. I think I have an important story. I'm a unique individual. I've done a lot of things that other people can't afford. I'm spending about $8,000 a month on shit to keep me alive.

A person with pancreatic cancer usually lives about six months. I'm writing this in July 2009, and I've been here twenty-two months. Will I make it to twenty-six or twenty-eight? I don't know. I have no idea. But I am hoping to see this book come out.

The point is that it can be possible to get more time. Does it fuck me up not to know when? No. If I died now or died seven months from now, what difference would it make? None. For me, personally, none. To me, death is final. I don't believe in anything else beyond that. That's it. Game over.

I had this crazy nut of a mechanic a long time ago. His name was Herman — he was killed a while ago. He was a fucked-up guy — a really fucked-up guy. Frank and I used to go to him because he was good with foreign cars. I had my MG and Frank had an Opel. One day I went to him after I had tried to fix my own brakes and he put me in a headlock, right there in the garage. That was the way he was. He put me into a sleeper hold and I was out, just like that. I woke up from that experience thinking that if that was what death was going to be like, then I'm not afraid of it. It was just like going to sleep.

I have the gravy now. The thing is that I have had a wonderful, great life, and the group of people who are going to be affected includes everybody in my life but me. When I die, I die. I'm gone. It's like being born. You have no idea of it happening. Imagine being conscious and aware when that happens. Holy shit.

What I'm trying to do is leave a legacy and an impression of who Mischa Weisz is. I'm hoping that in the future when people look back on my life, they'll remember a person who found a way to get the best out of everything, including problems. I hope they'll see that even if you die from cancer, you can still win in the process. A lot of people don't think that way. They get cancer and they prepare to die. Not a lot of people fight, and if they do fight, they work with limited information. They could fight more if they had more cancer information. Fewer people would get cancer in the first place if they had more information and followed it, especially when it comes to diet. We all know that if we don't take care of ourselves, we're going to get cancer and die, but until we actually get cancer, most of us do fuck all about it.

The thing about checking out at fifty-three or fifty-four, or whenever this happens, is that I can honestly say I have had a wonderful life. I sometimes wonder if I lived another ten years, what the hell would I do anyway? I am at the prime of my life. I would rather go now than be stuck in some stupid little home where my children come and see me every six months and ask, "How are you doing, Dad?" while I sit there all hunched over and shaking, trying to get my soup spoon up to my mouth. I couldn't do that. I just couldn't.

I am so happy with what I have done, between my kids, my friends, the experiences I have had in life and in business. I've done it all. What am I going to do: paint by numbers for the rest of my life? Sit on boards for charities and waste more of my life, listening to endless rhetoric and bullshit? I don't have the patience or stupidity. To use an old line, life is short. People don't always appreciate every single day, and suddenly they're fifty years old and they're alone. I see a lot of that in people. I don't see as many happy people as I would like to see.

⚬═✦═⚬

I know this is going to sound strange, but I ask: does it make a difference if you die at ten or die at ninety? Not necessarily. If you live all your life and leave nothing — you have no children, you work as someone else's employee, and you drop dead — was your life really worth anything? If I did nothing interesting with my life and then dropped dead I would have brought no growth to society. You have to do something, you have to participate, you have to be part of society and help it grow.

If you don't use your life to do something worth remembering, then, in my opinion, it wasn't that important. I think everybody has a duty to make something worthwhile out of their lives, and to help society in some way that people remember. One of the things I will have on my gravestone is, "As long as my name is spoken, I will still be alive." Once your name is forgotten, you're gone.

When I go to the cancer clinic, for example, I admire these little old ladies and old men who volunteer there. They're helping other people, doing something constructive that matters, and that other people will remember.

I've had a few friends who haven't done anything in their lives: they don't even read books or go to the movies. They just do their jobs. I don't get it. I don't understand how they're living.

We have one chance to be here and how we play this game to the end is what it's all about. Some people just don't grasp life, understand it, or enjoy it. I can honestly say that I have enjoyed my life. Even sitting at the casino in front of a stupid machine pushing buttons — winning some and losing a lot — I have had fun.

The life that I've been having since my diagnosis, particularly since the time I was projected to have died, is my victory over cancer. In this time I have been able to bring peace and closure to a lot of parts of my life: in my business, with my kids, my friends, my brother and his family. I have tried to do it with my parents, but that may simply be too complicated for all of us after all this time. At least we are on good terms and we know we love one another.

Frank and Linda were always there. Frank especially has been there, through everything — through all of my businesses and in my life. Our lives have been intertwined for more than forty years. We're like Arnold Schwarzenegger and Danny DeVito in *Twins*. That's what people used to tease us about. He is conservative and careful, while I am spontaneous and enjoy taking risks. We both have the capacity to care about things very much and that is our common link. Frank has been rallying behind me since I got sick, and I'm sure he'll be one of the people most hurt when I die. We've been talking every day for more than forty years, and how do you get over a relationship like that?

Paul and I have known each other nearly as long, even though we had that eight year break where we didn't talk to each other. When I got sick, we started to talk again. Shit happens.

<hr />

I'm generally okay. I continue to believe that there has got to be a way to treat this cancer. I am always asking, what have I missed? There has got to be a way. There always has been, in my business, in my family. Even if takes years, there has always been a solution.

There's one other thing. It doesn't haunt me, but it bothers me, because I'm not sure what's right or wrong sometimes. I hope I did the right thing letting my kids move away at such a young age. The thing is, I brought up my kids to be very independent. They live on their own and they're seeking to be entrepreneurs, which is kind of cool. I ask myself what would be better: that they live on their own and I pass away, or that they are still living at home and I pass away. I ask which scenario is better for them, and I think it's better for them not to be here at home, because what you don't see every day you're not going to miss as much. I am trying to protect my children by living my last days apart from them. If they were at home they'd be seeing me every day and suddenly I wouldn't be there. I think they're going to be hurt when I die, but I think they'd be a lot more hurt if they were living here.

It's also the best thing for me. My choice to be on my own a lot is to try to be in touch with my body, to meditate, to fight my disease without a lot of distractions. Emotionally, I think my kids are in a safer place this way than they would be if they were here with me. I think about it a lot. Have I done it the right way? Have I done it the wrong way?

Then I listen to my daughter on the phone, and she's having fun and enjoying her life. That's all that's important to me. My job is to raise these children and then let them go and do their own thing. When they do well, their happiness is my reward. If my daughter gets a contract with a film studio to do makeup, and she's happy about it, then I'd be in heaven.

It's a bad time in their lives for me to go, just as they are becoming independent. It's a time when young people enjoy their lives, but don't necessarily appreciate them and all they can be. I don't think Danielle and Nathan will appreciate what they have until they're in their thirties and forties, which is completely natural. It will happen with maturity and time, as it does for everyone. It's like paintings; they get their value with time. You see a painting now and it's good, but a hundred years from now people will say, "Wow!"

This book is something I hope they will appreciate, like a good wine, when they're in their later twenties, thirties, and forties. As they look for their own answers, they may flip through the pages and say, "Oh, Dad handled it that way," or "That's how Dad was." I hope that when they're missing me they'll read it, and it will be like talking to me. It's a way of communicating with my kids.

I would dearly love to see my kids get older, and I wish I could be there to help them when they need it, and to celebrate their accomplishments with them. I'd love to be there when they get married, and I'd love to be a grand-father. Those are some of life's richest moments. But is it going to happen? No. I love my children very much. That is very important to me and I want them to know that, and I think they do.

I've set up something very different for my kids for after I die. I struggled for a long time over how to handle their inheritance. Should I give them nothing? Should I give it all to charity and let them struggle the way I did? I wanted to do the right thing, something that would help them while also bringing out the best in them. I rejected every traditional way of doing it.

Reaching out from the grave is very hard to do. I could leave them each a fortune from day one. But what good would that do? They don't have an appreciation of money and they would probably blow it. I want them to still feel like their dad is here. I want to stay in their lives, every day. I want them to think about me every day. I know that may be selfish, but I want to be involved.

Then I found a balance. I set up their inheritance in the form of wage matching.

The best way I could see to stay in their lives was to set it up so that at the end of every year they would have to say, "Look, Dad! I made $30,000. Match it." If they go to school, I'll pay them $25,000 a year. If they go off to have a baby, they'll get $50,000 a year. My lawyer looked at me like I was up the wall when I asked him to set it up, but to me it's simple. It's straightforward. It's a way to stay in their lives. I'm very happy with that. When I told my children, they didn't say anything, but I could see they didn't like it much.

I know they'll get it one day. I don't look to get a lot back from my children. I want to feel I've done a good job, and I know these kids are well taken care of. If I'm sad about anything it's that I can't be there for them down the road. When they need somebody to talk to, I won't be there for them.

I'm on my own a lot these days, but I am never lonely. I have lots of friends, and I have Connie and my family. If I want to go out golfing or to the casino, or to a show, or go away for a few days, I can.

I still take my camera when I go somewhere. I look at my camera sometimes, and I ask myself, "Why are you doing this? You're not going to be here in five years to look at the pictures." I still do it. I hope my kids will look at them.

What we want to do with the new treatment is get that cancer marker back down. Right now it's increasing by ten or twelve points a day. We're probably up to four hundred in the week since I had my last count done. By the time I get the new treatment, it'll be closer to one thousand. I'm not close to death, but I am starting to sense the light at the end of the tunnel that I don't want to see yet. The idea is that this stuff will knock the marker completely down.

How many people have fifty-seven chemos? How many people live two years with pancreatic cancer? Not many. There's nothing to compare this situation to.

I have kept really close to my diet lately, but yesterday I cheated. I had a bun with roast beef. Sometimes I need that energy, that protein, something substantial. Cancer just robs your energy, and once in a while some protein seems to bring it back a little.

I had a really good sleep last night and that was good. I love my sleep. If sleep and death are the same thing, then I have nothing to worry about. I'll be happy, as long as I don't have to get up and pee.

EPILOGUE

Mischa Weisz died October 2, 2009. He was fifty-three years old and had survived for nearly twenty-five months since learning he could expect to live only five. During that time he lived on his own terms, just as he had his entire life.

Mischa had planned to spend September 11, 2009 — the second anniversary of his diagnosis — riding in a limousine on a tour of local charities, handing out a cheque at every stop, as a way of celebrating the extra time he had been granted.

Illness forced him to postpone the tour, but he never cancelled it. He held onto the hope that he would be able to enjoy his day of giving once he felt better.

By that time, the cancer was spreading exponentially and inexorably though his body, leaving him exhausted, uncomfortable, and unable to eat. September 11 turned out to be the day he was released from hospital for the last time.

In his determination to continue living, several days earlier he chose to have major surgery to remove portions of his intestine. While in hospital, Mischa watched an early copy of the documentary he had commissioned. The well-made film catalogues the medical odyssey that had brought him to that point, and he proudly showed it to visitors on a portable player in his room.

By then he had also reviewed and approved the edited text of this book, and was proud to have completed an important piece of his legacy.

He returned from hospital weak, but continued to make plans. He was eager to build up enough strength for one last road trip. He was planning to ride in a motor home to his beloved Port Elgin — if he could make it — to have one last campfire. A thirty-eight-foot luxury model was booked to arrive October 2.

As he had wished, he spent his final weeks at home, where Connie, Danielle, Nathan, and other family members and friends kept up his care and his spirits, aided by a team of dedicated medical personnel.

As long as he could, Mischa continued updating the blog he had kept about his experience with cancer, never changing the opening banner, "Rule No. 1: Don't Let A Diagnosis Slow You Down." When Mischa could no longer write, Connie wrote for him.

Mischa died hours before the motor home arrived. The next night, his closest friends and family carried on without him, driving to a scenic spot to tell stories and toast his memory.

The funeral that was held the following week was packed. Mischa had arranged for the service to be held at the First Unitarian Church of Hamilton — the same church that had once been located in a house next door to his parents' home. The congregation's new, and much larger, home, just blocks away from the original site, was barely big enough for the approximately 350 attendees, whose cars crammed every corner of the parking lot.

Mischa's family sat in the front pew, his photo smiling at them from a vantage point over his gleaming casket.

Frank Helt's eulogy, drawn from forty years of friendship, left members of the congregation alternately laughing and dabbing at tears.

"Mischa was like an old sweater that you got when you were a kid, one that you always had, that was comfortable and familiar, and even though it had some wear marks, and was not appropriate for every occasion, and not everybody liked it, it was yours, and no one else needed to understand why you kept it," he said. "That sweater was the unusual boy next door I was proud to call my friend."

Paul Buckle, seated with an acoustic guitar, introduced his performance of James Taylor's sad yet hopeful song, *(You Can) Close Your Eyes*, by describing the way Mischa had viewed his life as a line intersecting with the lines of other lives, each changing the course of the others'. Mischa's son, Nathan, and Paul's eldest, Daryl, plugged in electric guitars to join Paul for a jazzy instrumental version of *Amazing Grace*.

Mischa left several million dollars in new gifts to charity, including a significant donation to the Juravinski Cancer Centre, where he was treated. Most of his charitable bequest has been placed with a foundation, where the income will continue providing gifts to his designated charities in perpetuity.

Mischa Weisz knew that he was investing in a future he would never see.

— *Wade Hemsworth, October 2009,*
Hamilton, Ontario.